KEY FACTS KEY CASES

English Legal System

Jacqueline Martin

 Routledge
Taylor & Francis Group

LONDON AND NEW YORK

First published 2014
by Routledge
2 Park Square, Milton Park, Abingdon, Oxon OX14 4RN

and by Routledge
711 Third Avenue, New York, NY 10017

Routledge is an imprint of the Taylor & Francis Group, an informa business

© 2014 Jacqueline Martin

British Library Cataloguing in Publication Data
A catalogue record for this book is available from the British Library

Library of Congress Cataloging in Publication Data
A catalog record for this book has been requested.

ISBN: 978–0–415–83326–4 (pbk)
ISBN: 978–1–315–87965–9 (ebk)

Typeset in Helvetica
by RefineCatch Limited, Bungay, Suffolk

Contents

PREFACE   x

TABLE OF CASES   xii

Chapter 1

WHAT IS LAW?   1

1.1   The nature of law   1
1.2   Classification of law   2
1.3   Distinctions between civil and criminal law   4
      Key Cases Checklist   5

Chapter 2

JUDICIAL PRECEDENT   7

2.1   The doctrine of precedent   8
2.2   Hierarchy of the courts   10
2.3   The House of Lords and the Practice Statement   11
2.4   The Supreme Court   13
2.5   The position of the Court of Appeal   14
2.6   *Ratio* and *obiter*   16
2.7   Distinguishing   17
2.8   Advantages and disadvantages of precedent   17
2.9   Judicial law-making in precedent   18
      Key Cases Checklist   19

Chapter 3

LEGISLATION   36

3.1   Acts of Parliament   36
3.2   The process in Parliament   38
3.3   Advantages of statute law over case law   40
3.4   Parliamentary sovereignty   40
3.5   Delegated legislation   41
      Key Cases Checklist   44

Chapter 4

STATUTORY INTERPRETATION   48

4.1   Need for statutory interpretation   49
4.2   Approaches to statutory interpretation   49
4.3   Results of interpretation   50
4.4   The purposive approach   51
4.5   Intrinsic aids   51
4.6   Extrinsic aids   51
4.7   Rules of language   52
4.8   Presumptions   53
4.9   The European approach   53
4.10 The effect of the Human Rights Act 1998   54
4.11 The judicial role in interpretation   54
      Key Cases Checklist   55

Chapter 5

EUROPEAN UNION LAW   71

5.1   The institutions   72
5.2   Sources of law   74
5.3   Effect on sovereignty of Parliament   76
      Key Cases Checklist   78

Chapter 6

LAW REFORM   83

6.1   The need for law reform   84
6.2   Law Commission   84
6.3   Other law reform bodies   86

Chapter 7

THE CIVIL JUSTICE SYSTEM   87

7.1   The court structure   88
7.2   Procedure in outline   89
7.3   Encouraging ADR   91
7.4   Appeals   91
7.5   Comment on the post-Woolf civil system   93
7.6   Alternative dispute resolution   94
      Key Cases Checklist   96

Chapter 8

TRIBUNALS AND INQUIRIES   103

8.1   Administrative tribunals   103
8.2   Control of tribunals   105
8.3   Domestic tribunals   106
8.4   Inquiries   107
       Key Cases Checklist   108

Chapter 9

POLICE POWERS   109

9.1   Stop and search   110
9.2   Searching premises   111
9.3   Powers of arrest   112
9.4   Detention at the police station   115
9.5   Complaints against the police   118
       Key Cases Checklist   119

Chapter 10

THE CRIMINAL PROCESS AND COURTS   126

10.1   The Crown Prosecution Service (CPS)   127
10.2   Bail   127
10.3   Classification of offences   129
10.4   Magistrates' Court   129
10.5   Appeals from the Magistrates' Court   131
10.6   The Crown Court   132
10.7   Appeals from the Crown Court   132
10.8   Miscarriages of justice   134
       Key Materials   134

Chapter 11

SENTENCING   136

11.1   Aims of sentencing   137
11.2   Types of sentences   140
11.3   Other powers of the court   142
11.4   Additional powers in respect of young offenders (10–17) 142
11.5   Mentally ill offenders   143
11.6   Other factors in sentencing   143

Chapter 12

THE LEGAL PROFESSION   145

12.1   Solicitors   146
12.2   Barristers   147
12.3   Queen's Counsel   148
12.4   Para-legals   149
12.5   Regulation of the legal professions   149
12.6   Legal Services Act 2007   150
       Key Cases Checklist   151

Chapter 13

THE JUDICIARY   154

13.1   Appointment   155
13.2   Training   157
13.3   Removal   157
13.4   Independence of the Judiciary   158
13.5   The Lord Chancellor's role   159
       Key Cases Checklist   160

Chapter 14

LAY MAGISTRATES   163

14.1   Qualifications   163
14.2   Appointment   164
14.3   Composition of the Bench   164
14.4   Training   165
14.5   Retirement and removal   165
14.6   Role   166
14.7   Advantages   166
14.8   Disadvantages   167
       Key Cases Checklist   167

Chapter 15

JURIES   170

15.1   Use of juries   171
15.2   Jury qualifications   171
       Key Cases Checklist   176

Chapter 16

LEGAL SERVICES AND FUNDING   190

16.1   Public funding for civil cases   190
16.2   Private funding for civil cases   192
16.3   Advice agencies   193
16.4   Legal aid in criminal cases   193

INDEX   195

Preface

The Key Facts Key Cases series is a practical and complete revision aid that can be used by students of law courses at all levels from A Level to degree and beyond, and in professional and vocational courses also.

The Key Facts Key Cases series is designed to give a clear view of each subject. This will be useful to students when tackling new topics and is invaluable as a revision aid.

Most chapters open with an outline in diagram form of the points covered in that chapter. The points are then developed in a structured list form to make learning easier. Supporting cases are given throughout by name and for some complex areas facts are given to reinforce the point being made.

The Key Facts Key Cases series aims to accommodate the syllabus content of most qualifications in a subject area, using many visual learning aids.

Each title in the Key Facts Key Cases series now incorporates a Key Cases section at the end of each chapter which is designed to give a clear understanding of important cases. This is useful when studying a new topic and invaluable as a revision aid. Each case is broken down into fact and law. In addition many cases are extended by the use of important extracts from the judgment or by comment or by highlighting problems. Cases marked in bold in the key facts section signify that they have then been included with further detail in the key cases checklist at the end of the chapter.

In some instances students are reminded that there is a link to other cases or material. If the link case is in another part of the book, the reference will be clearly shown. Links will be to additional cases or materials that do not feature in the book.

To give a clear layout, symbols have been used at the start of each component of the case. The symbols are:

 Key Facts – These are the basic facts of the case.

 Key Law – This is the major principle of law in the case.

Key Judgment – This is an actual extract from a judgment made on the case.

 Key Comment – Influential or appropriate comments made on the case.

 Key Problem – Apparent inconsistencies or difficulties in the law.

 Key Link – This indicates other cases which should be considered with this case.

The Key Link symbol alerts readers to links within the book and also to cases and other material especially statutory provisions which are not included.

The court abbreviations used in the key case sections of this book are shown below.

Ass	Assize Court	CA	Court of Appeal
CC	County Court	CCA	Court of Criminal Appeal
CCR	Crown Cases Reserved	CH	Court of Chancery
ChDiv	Chancery Division	CJEU	Court of Justice of the European Union
C-MAC	Court Martial Appeal Court	CP	Court of Probate
DC	Divisional Court	EAT	Employment Appeal Tribunal
ECHR	European Court of Human Rights	ECJ	European Court of Justice
ET/IT	Employment tribunal/Industrial tribunal	Exch	Court of the Exchequer
HC	High Court	HL	House of Lords
KBD	King's Bench Division	NIRC	National Industrial Relations Court
PC	Privy Council	QBD	Queen's Bench Division
RC	Rolls Court	SC	Supreme Court

The law is as I believe it to be on 1 July 2013.

Table of Cases

Addie (Robert) & Sons (Collieries Ltd) v Dumbreck [1929]
 AC 358 .... 12, 24
Agricultural, Horticultural and Forestry Industrial Training
 Board v Aylesbury Mushrooms Ltd [1972] 1 All ER 280 .... 43, 44, 46
Airedale NHS Trust v Bland [1993] 1 WLR 316 .... 1, 5
Adler v George [1964] 1 All ER 628 .... 50, 55, 59
Allen v Emmerson [1944] KB 362, [1944] All ER 344 .... 52, 69
Anderton v Clwyd County Council [2002] EWCA Civ 933,
 [2002] 3 All ER 813 102
Anderton v Ryan [1985] 2 All ER 355 .... 12, 24–5
Anns v London Borough of Merton [1978] AC 728 12
Attorney-General v Guardian Newspapers Ltd (Spycatcher case)
 [1987] 3 All ER 316, [1987] 1 WLR 1248, HL, *affirming*
 [1987] 3 All ER 316, CA 159
Attorney-General for Jersey v Holley [2005] 2 AC 580, [2005]
 3 All ER 371 33
Attorney-General's Reference (No 4 of 2002), *see*
 Sheldrake v DPP—
Automatic Telephone and Electric Co Ltd v Registrar of
 Restrictive Trading Agreements [1965] 1 All ER 206 .... 8, 19, 20
Avery v Scott (1853) 8 Exch 497 91
Aylesbury Mushrooms case, *see* Agricultural, Horticultural
 and Forestry Industrial Training Board v Aylesbury
 Mushrooms Ltd—

Baldwin v Ridge, *see* Ridge v Baldwin—
Balfour v Balfour [1919] 2 KB 571 .... 17, 32–3
Beamish v Beamish (1861) 9 HL Cas 274,
 8 Jur NS 770 11
Black-Clawson International Ltd v Papierwerke
 Waldhof-Aschaffenburg AG [1975] AC 591, [1975]
 1 All ER 810 .... 52, 64, 65
Boys v Chaplin [1969] 3 WLR 322, [1968] 1 All ER 283 15
British Railways Board v Pickin [1974] 1 All ER 609 .... 40, 44, 45

Brock v DPP (1993) *The Times*, 23 July 49

Broome v Cassell & Co Ltd [1972] 1 All ER 801,
    HL, [1971] 2 QB 354, [1971] 2 All ER 187, CA 11, 14, 19, 21–2, 27

Burchell v Bullard [2005] EWCA Civ 358....................................91, 96, 101

Bushell's Case (1670) Vaugh 135 ....174, 183, 185–6

C v DPP [1995] 2 All ER 43..19, 32, 35

Cable & Wireless plc v IBM [2002] EWHC
    2059 Comm..91, 96, 99

Central Asbestos Co Ltd v Dodd [1973]
    AC 518, [1972] 2 All ER 1135 17

Central London Property Ltd v High Trees House Ltd
    [1947] KB 130..17

Charles v Crown Prosecution Service [2009]
    EWHC 3521 (Admin) 116, 119, 124

Colchester Estates (Cardiff) v Carlton Industries plc
    [1984] 2 All ER 601 11

Commission v UK, *Re* Tachograph [1979] ECR 419.................74, 75, 78, 80

Conway v Rimmer [1968] AC 910, [1968] 1 All ER 874 12

Costa v ENEL [1964] CMLR 425 76

Davis v Johnson [1979] AC 264, [1978]
    2 WLR 553, [1978] 1 All ER 1132 ....12, 14, 16, 26, 29

Director General of Fair Trading v The Proprietary Association
    of Great Britain [2001] 1 WLR 700....................15, 27, 106, 108, 159–61

DPP v Bull [1994] 4 All ER 411...50, 62, 65

DPP for Northern Ireland v Lynch [1975] AC 653 12

Donoghue v Stevenson [1932] AC 562 32

Dori v Recreb Srl (Case C-91/92) [1994] ECR I-3325,
    [1995] All ER (EC) 1 ....75, 76

Dowling, *Re* [1967] 1 AC 725..12

Duke v GEC Reliance Ltd [1988] AC 618, [1988]
    1 All ER 626..74, 75, 78, 80–1

Duncan v Cammell Laird and Co Ltd [1942]
    AC 624, [1942] 1 All ER 587, HL..12

Dunnett v Railtrack plc [2002] EWCA Civ
    303, [2002] 2 All ER 850...91, 96, 99–100, 101

Eastbourne Borough Council v Stirling [2000]
    EWHC Admin 410, (2000) *The Times*, 16 November 61

Fisher v Bell [1960] 1 QB 394...50, 56

Fitzpatrick v Sterling Housing Association [2001] 1 AC 27.......................27

Foster v British Gas plc [1990] IRLR 353 75
Fothergill v Monarch Airlines Ltd [1980]
    3 WLR 209, [1980] 2 All ER 696 ....52, 64, 66
Francovich v Italian Republic [1991] ECR-I 5357 ....74, 76

Ghaidan v Godin-Mendoza [2004] UKHL 30, [2004]
    3 All ER 411, HL, *affirming* [2002] EWCA Civ
    1533,CA 15, 26, 27, 54
Gillan v United Kingdom: Quinton v United Kingdom
    [2010] Crim LR 415 ....119, 120–1
Godwin v Swindon Borough Council [2001] EWCA
    Civ 1478, [2001] 4 All ER 641 101–2
Goldsmith v Pressdram Ltd [1987] 3 All ER 485......................171, 176, 180
Grey v Pearson (1857) 6 HL Cas 61 ....50, 55, 58–9
Grimaldi v Fond des Maladies Professionelles [1989]
    ECR 4407 ....74, 76, 78, 81

H v Ministry of Defence [1991] 2 WLR 1192, [1991]
    2 All ER 834...171, 176, 179
Hall, Arthur JS & Co (a firm) v Simons [2000]
    3 WLR 543, [2000] 3 All ER 673 ....150, 151, 153
Halsey v Milton Keynes General NHS Trust [2004]
    EWCA Civ 576 ....91, 96, 100, 101
Hanif v United Kingdom 52999/08 (2012) 55 EHRR
    16, [2012] Crim LR 295..172, 176, 182
Hayes v Chief Constable of Merseyside [2011] EWCA
    Civ 911 ....113, 119, 122–3
Henn and Derby v DPP [1981] AC 850, [1980]
    2 All ER 166, HL..53
Herrington v British Railways Board [1972] AC 877................12, 18, 19, 24
Heydon's Case (1584) 3 Co Rep 7a 50, 55, 60
High Trees case, *see* Central London Property Ltd v High
    Trees House Ltd [1947] KB 130—
Hobbs v CG Robertson Ltd [1970] 1 WLR 980..........................52, 64, 68–9
Hodges v Harland & Wolff [1965] 1 All ER 1086 ....171, 178
Huddersfield Police Authority v Watson [1947]
    2 All ER 193...11
Hulton & Co v Jones [1910] AC 20 21
Hunter and others v Canary Wharf Ltd and London
    Dockland Development Corporation [1996]
    1 All ER 482, [1995] NLJR 1645..8

Inland Revenue Commissioners v Frere [1965] AC 402 ....52, 64, 70

Internationale Handelsgesellschaft mbH v Einfuhr und Vorratsstelle
   für Getreide und Futtermittel (Case 11/70) [1970] ECR 1125,
   [1972] CMLR 255 77

Jones v Secretary of State for Social Services [1972] AC 944 ....12, 13
Jones v Tower Boot Co Ltd [1997] 3 All ER 406 ....51, 55, 63

KS v R [2010] EWCA Crim 1756 ....171, 176, 177
Kadhim v Brent London Borough Council (2001) *Times*,
   27 March 9
Kammins Ballroom Co Ltd v Zenith Investments (Torquay)
   Ltd [1971] AC 850, [1970] 2 All ER 871 54
Kleinwort Benson Ltd v Lincoln City Council [1998]
   4 All ER 513 ....8, 19, 20–1

Lawal v Northern Spirit Ltd [2003] UKHL 35 ....159, 160, 162
Lees v Secretary of State for Social Services [1985]
   AC 930, [1985] 2 All ER 203 50
Leonesio v Ministero dell'Agricoltura (Case 93/71) [1972]
   ECR 287, [1973] CMLR 343, ECJ 74, 75
Ley v Hamilton (1935) 79 Sol Jo 573, 153 LT 384 21
London and North Eastern Railway Co v Berriman [1946]
   AC 278, [1946] 1 All ER 255 ....50, 55, 57
London Tramways v London County Council [1898]
   AC 375 11

Macarthys Ltd v Smith (Case 129/79) [1981] QB 180,
   [1981] 1 All ER 111, CA, *applying* [1980] ECR 1275,
   ECJ, *referred from* [1979] 1 WLR 1189, CA, *on appeal
   from* [1978] 2 All ER 746, EAT 74, 75, 78, 79
McLeod v Commissioner of Police of the Metropolis
   [1994] 4 All ER 553 111
Magor and St Mellons RDC v Newport Corporation
   [1950] 2 All ER 1226 ....54, 55, 58
Marshall v Southampton and South West Hampshire
   Area Health Authority [1986] 2 ECR 723, [1986]
   2 All ER 584 ....74, 75, 78, 80, 81
Mendoza v Ghaidan [2002] EWCA Civ 1533 ....15, 26, 27, 54
Merritt v Merritt [1970] 1 WLR 1211, [1970]
   2 All ER 760, CA 17, 32, 34
Metropolitan Police Commissioner v Caldwell [1981]
   1 All ER 961, [1982] AC 341, HL, *affirming*
   R v Caldwell (1980) 71 Cr App R 237, CA............................13, 25, 65–6

Michaels v Highbury Corner Magistrates' Court [2009]
     EWHC 2928 (Admin) 120
Miliangos v George Frank (Textiles) Ltd [1975]
     3 All ER 801, HL, [1976] AC 443, [1975]
     1 All ER 1076. CA 11, 14, 15, 19, 22–3, 26, 27
Murphy v Brentwood District Council [1991]
     1 AC 398, [1990] 2 All ER 908 12

O'Loughlin v Chief Constable of Essex [1998]
     1 WLR 374 .... 112, 119, 121–2
Osman v DPP (1999) *The Times*, 28 September 110, 119, 120

Pepper (Inspector of Taxes) v Hart [1993]
     1 All ER 42 .... 12, 51, 53, 54, 64, 67
Pinochet Ugarte, *Re, see* R v Bow Street Magistrates,
     ex parte Pinochet Ugarte (No 2)—
Ponting's case, *see* R v Ponting (Clive)—
Practice Direction (Magistrates: Clerk and Authorised
     Legal Adviser) [2000] 4 All ER 895 .... 166, 167, 169
Practice Note (Jury: Stand by: Jury Checks) [1988]
     3 All ER 1086 173
Practice Statement (Judicial Precedent) [1966]
     3 All ER 77 .... 19, 23

R (on the application of Ghai) v Newcastle upon Tyne
     City Council (Ramgharia Gurdwara, Hitchin intervening)
     [2010] EWCA Civ 59, [2011] QB 591, CA 55
R (on the application of Quintavalle) v Secretary of State
     for Health [2003] 2 All ER 113, [2003] UKHL
     13, HL 51, 55, 63–4
R (on the application of S and Marper) v United Kingdom,
     see S v United Kingdom: Marper v United Kingdom—
R v Abdroikov [2007] UKHL 37, [2008] 1 All ER 315, HL,
     reversing in part [2005] EWCA Crim 1986, CA 172, 176, 181
R v Adomako [1995] 1 AC 171, [1994] 3 All ER 79, HL 13
R v Alladice (1988) 87 Cr App Rep 380, [1988]
     Crim LR 608, CA 116
R v Altrincham Justices, *ex parte* Pennington [1975]
     QB 549, [1975] 2 All ER 78, QBD 106
R v Aspinall [1999] 2 Cr App Rep 115, (1999)
     The Times, 4 February 116, 119, 123–4
R v Badham [1987] Crim LR 202 112
R v Bliss (1986) 84 Cr App R 1 181

R v Bow Street Magistrates, *ex parte* Pinochet Ugarte (No 2)
[1999] 1 All ER 577 ....159, 160–1
R v Caldwell, *see* Metropolitan Police Commissioner v Caldwell—
R v Chairman of Stephen Lawrence Inquiry, *ex parte* A
(1998) *Times*, 25 July 107
R v Connor; R v Mirza (conjoined appeals) [2004]
UKHL 4 ....175, 183, 188–9
R v Cunningham [1957] 2 QB 396 66
R v Eccles Justices, *ex parte* Fitzpatrick (1989) 89 Cr
App Rep 324 166–8
R v Ford [1989] 3 All ER 445 ....173, 183, 185
R v G and R [2003] UKHL 50, [2004]
1 AC 1034 ....13, 19, 25, 53, 64–5
R v Gearing [1968] 1 WLR 344 189
R v Gotts [1992] 2 AC 412 [1992] 1 All ER 832 9
R v Gough [1993] AC 658 161
R v Gould [1968] 2 QB 65, [1968] 1 All ER 849 ....14, 16, 26, 31
R v HM Treasury, *ex parte* British Telecommunications
plc [1996] QB 615 76
R v Halliwell [2012] EWCA Crim 2924, [2013]
2 Cr App Rep (S) 261 ....116, 119, 125
R v Howe [1987] 2 WLR 568 ....9, 12
R v James: R v Karimi [2006] EWCA Crim 14 ....15, 29–30, 32, 33
R v Jenkins [1983] 1 All ER 1000, 76 Cr App
R 313, CA 16
R v Judge of the City of London Court [1892]
1 QB 273 ....50, 55, 56
R v Kansal (No 2) [2001] UKHL 62, [2002]
2 AC 69, HL 13
R v Karakaya [2005] EWCA Crim 346 ....183, 189
R v Longman [1988] 1 WLR 619, [1988] Crim LR 534 ....112, 119, 121
R v McCann (1990) 154 JP 917 173
R v McKenna [1960] 1 QB 411 ....174, 183, 186
R v Mason [1980] 3 All ER 777 ....170, 173, 183, 184–5
R v Mirza, *see* R v Connor; R v Mirza (conjoined appeals)—
R v Pigg [1983] 1 All ER 56 ....174, 183, 186–7
R v Ponting (Clive) [1985] Crim LR 318 174
R v R (Rape: Marital Exemption) [1991]
4 All ER 481 ....19, 32, 34–5, 84
R v R and G, *see* R v G and R—
R v Randle, R v Pottle [1991] 1WLR 1087 174
R v Richardson [2004] EWCA Crim 2997 ....171, 176, 180–1
R v Samuel [1988] QB 615, [1988] 2 All ER 135 ....116, 119, 123

R v Secretary of State for Education and Employment, *ex parte*
National Union of Teachers [2000] All ER (D) 991, (2000)
The Times, 8 August 43, 46–7
R v Secretary of State for the Home Office, *ex parte* Brind [1991]
2 WLR 588, CA 159
R v Secretary of State for the Home Office,
ex parte Fire Brigades Union [1995]
2 All ER 244..43, 44, 46
R v Secretary of State for Transport, *ex parte* Factortame
(Case C-213/89) [1990] ECR 1-2433, [1991]
1 All ER 70...3, 41, 44, 45, 71, 77, 78, 81–2
R v Seymour [1983] 2 AC 493, [1983]
2 All ER 1058...13
R v Sheffield Crown Court, *ex parte* Brownlow [1980]
2 All ER 444..173, 183–4
R v Shivpuri [1986] 2 All ER 334 ....12, 19, 24–5
R v Simpson [2003] EWCA 1499 6
R v Smith (Morgan James) [2001] 1 AC 146.....................................33
R v Spencer [1986] 2 All ER 928, [1986] 3 WLR 348,
HL, *affirming* [1985] 1 All ER 673, CA 16, 26, 32
R v Sussex Justices, *ex parte* McCarthy [1924] 1 KB 256.....................166–8
R v Taylor [1950] 2 KB 368...11, 16
R v Thompson [1962] 1 All ER 65..183, 187
R v Twomey (John) and others [2009] EWCA Crim 1035,
(2009) *Times*, 25 June..171, 175, 176–7
R v Wheat: R v Stocks [1921] 2 KB 119..31
R v Young (Stephen) [1995] 2 WLR 430, [1995]
QB 324 ....170, 174, 183, 187–8
Racz v Home Office [1994] 2 WLR 23 ....176, 179
Rakhit v Carty [1990] 2 All ER 202..16, 31
Richardson v The Chief Constable of West Midlands
Police [2011] EWHC 773 (QB)..113, 125
Rickards v Rickards [1989] 3 WLR 748, [1989]
3 All ER 193..16, 26, 30–1
Ridge v Baldwin [1963] 2 All ER 66 ....106, 108
Roberts Petroleum Ltd v Bernard Kenny Ltd [1983]
2 AC 192, [1983] 1 All ER 564, HL..10
Rondel v Worsley [1967] 3 All ER 993, [1969]
1 AC 191 ....150, 153
Rookes v Barnard [1964] AC 1129 ....14, 21
Ross v Caunters [1979] 3 WLR 605..150, 151–2
Royal College of Nursing v DHSS [1981]
1 All ER 545, [1982] AC 800 ....49, 50, 55, 61–2

S v United Kingdom: Marper v United Kingdom
    (Applications 30562/04 and 30566/04) (2008)
    48 EHRR 1169, [2009] Crim LR 355, ECtHR 118, 119, 124–5
Saif Ali v Sydney Mitchell and Co [1980] AC 198,
    [1978] 3 WLR 849 150
Sander v United Kingdom [2000] Crim LR 767,
    (2000) *The Times*, 12 May 170, 174, 188
Schorsch Meier GmbH v Hennin [1975]
    1 QB 416, [1975] 1 All ER 152 .... 14, 22–3, 26
Schweppes Ltd v Registrar of Restrictive Trading
    Agreements [1965] 1 All ER 195 .... 8, 20
Scott v Avery (1856) 5 HL Cas 811 .... 95, 96, 98–9
Sheldrake v Director of Public Prosecutions; Attorney
    General's Reference (No 4 of 2002) [2004]
    UKHL 43, [2005] 1 All ER 237 54
Sigsworth, *Re* [1935] Ch 89 .... 50, 55, 59–60
Simmenthal SpA v EC Commission (No 2) (Case 92/78)
    [1979] ECR 777, [1980] 1 CMLR 25 77
Sirros v Moore [1975] QB 118, CA 159
Smith v Hughes [1960] 2 All ER 859 .... 50, 55, 60–1
Strickland v Hayes Borough Council [1896]
    1 QB 290 .... 43, 44, 47
Swain v Hillman [1999] All ER (D) 1210 93

Tachographs, *Re, see* Commission v UK, *Re* Tachograph—
Tanfern Ltd v Cameron-Macdonald [2000]
    2 All ER 801 92
Taylor v Chief Constable of Thames Valley Police [2004]
    EWCA Civ 1022 .... 113, 119, 122
Tempest v Kilner (1846) 3 CB 249 .... 52, 64, 69
Three Rivers District Council and others v Bank of
    England (No 2) [1996] 2 All ER 363 52

United Railways of Havana and Regla Warehouses, *Re*
    [1960] 2 All ER 332, [1961] AC 100 .... 14, 22–3, 26

Van Duyn v Home Office [1974] ECR 1337, [1975]
    3 All ER 190 .... 74, 75, 78, 79
Van Gend en Loos v Nederlandse Administratie
    [1963] ECR 1 .... 71, 76, 78, 81
Vinos v Marks and Spencer plc [2001] 3 All ER 784 .... 91, 96, 98
Von Colson and Kamann v Land Nordrhein-Westfalen
    (Case 14/83) [1984] ECR 1891, [1986] 2 CMLR 430 53

Ward v James [1966] 1 QB 273, [1966]
   1 All ER 563 .... 171, 176, 177–8, 179
White v Jones [1995] 1 All ER 691 .... 150, 151, 152
Whiteley v Chappell (1868) 4 LR QB 147 .... 50, 55, 57
Williams v Fawcett [1985] 1 All ER 787,
   [1986] QB 604 .... 16, 26, 30
Wilson v First County Trust Ltd (No 2)
   [2003] UKHL 40 .... 51, 67–8

Young v Bristol Aeroplane Co Ltd [1944]
   KB 718, [1944] 2 All ER 293 .... 11, 15, 16, 26, 28, 31

1 What is law?

▶ 1.1 The nature of law

1.1.1 Definition of 'law'

A brief definition of 'law' is difficult, but the following are some suggestions.

1 Law is a set of rules that plays an important part in the creation and maintenance of social order.

2 John Austin defined law as a command issued from a Sovereign power to an inferior and enforced by coercion.

3 Sir John Salmond defined law as being 'the body of principles recognised and applied by the State in the administration of justice'.

4 Although law is a formal mechanism for controlling society, it is not the only mechanism; less formal rules of morality and custom also play a part.

1.1.2 Law and morality

1 Morality is what is right and wrong according to a set of values or beliefs governing a group's behaviour.

2 Morality is not fixed and will vary from one group/society to another. Moral values may also change over time.

3 Law and morality usually overlap on major issues, but may differ on other matters.

4 Murder is an example of an overlap. It is both legally and morally wrong. However, even on this major issue there are some who believe that euthanasia should be allowed, and legally it has been ruled that the withdrawal of sustenance from a person in a persistent vegetative state is not murder (*Airedale NHS Trust v Bland* (1993)).

5 Law and morality diverge on many issues. For example:

- abortion is legal under the Abortion Act 1967, but some groups believe it is morally wrong;

- smoking cannabis is legally wrong but many people believe it is not morally wrong.

6   Whether law and morality should be the same is a question that is debated. Positivists such as Hart and Kelsen state that law and morality are essentially separate, but proponents of the natural law theory (based on the theories of Aristotle and St. Thomas Aquinas) believe that law and morality should coincide.

1.1.3 A legal system

Professor Hart suggested five factors that he believed had to co-exist to create a legal system. These are:

a)   rules that forbid certain conduct and rules that compel certain conduct on pain of sanctions;

b)   rules requiring people to compensate those whom they injure;

c)   rules stating what needs to be done in certain 'mechanical' areas of law, such as making a contract or making a will;

d)   a system of courts to determine what the rules are, whether they have been broken, and what the appropriate sanction is;

e)   a body whose responsibility it is to make rules and amend or repeal them when necessary.

▶ 1.2 Classification of law

It is possible to classify law in many ways. For a law student, the most important ways are by:

- the type of law (ie the matters that the law is regulating);

- the source from which it comes; this affects the status of the law.

1.2.1 Classification by types of law

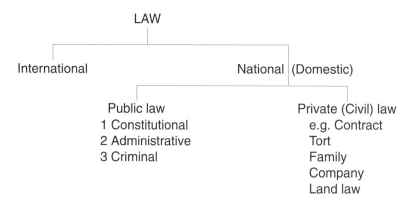

1   Law can be classified as international or national (domestic).

2   International law can be divided into public international law, which governs relationships between countries, and private international law, which governs which country's law should apply to individuals where there are links with at least two different countries. For example, which country's law should govern who inherits on a person's death.

3   National law can also be divided into public law and private law. Public law involves the State in some way, while private (civil) law controls the relationships between individuals.

4   National public law can be divided into:

- constitutional law;

- administrative law;

- criminal law.

5   National private law can be divided into many categories, including contract, tort, family, company, and land law.

1.2.2 Classification by source

1   European Union law is that which emanates from the Institutions of the EU. This can overrule national law (*R v Secretary of State for Transport, ex parte Factortame* (1991)).

2   Statutory law is that made by an Act of Parliament, eg Legal Aid, Sentencing and Punishment of Offenders Act 2012. Apart from EU law, statutory law is sovereign and cannot be challenged by the courts.

3   Regulatory law is secondary law made by delegated legislation.

4   Common law is law made by the decisions of the judges. It is also referred to as case law.

5   Equity law is law created by the Chancery courts under the Lord Chancellor to 'fill the gaps' in the common law. Although equity prevails over common law, equitable remedies are discretionary.

1.2.3 Different meanings of 'common law'

The phrase 'common law' is used in a number of ways, so it is important to be aware of the context in which it is used.

Different meanings	Distinguishes it from
Law developed by judges in the eleventh and twelfth centuries to form a 'common' law for the whole country	The local laws used prior to the Norman conquest
Judge-made law developed through judicial precedent	Laws made by a legislative body such as Acts of Parliament (statutory law)
The law operated in the common law courts before the reorganisation of the court structure in 1873–75	Equity – decisions of the Chancery courts
Common law systems – those following the English case-based system (mainly US and Commonwealth countries)	Civil law systems – those operated in European countries influenced by Roman law and which are largely code-based

▶ 1.3 Distinctions between civil and criminal law

Civil and criminal law have separate functions and operate in different courts. It is important to understand the differences.

	Civil	**Criminal**
Purpose	• Regulates relationships between individuals • Dispute settlement • Enforcement of rights	• Prevention of certain types of conduct • Enforcement of behaviour • Punishment of offenders
Courts	High Court County Court	Crown Court Magistrates' Court
Burden of proof	Balance of probability	Beyond reasonable doubt
Outcomes of cases	Liability decided Civil remedy awarded, eg • damages • injunction • declaration	Guilt or innocence decided Sentence imposed, eg • imprisonment • community order • fine
Terminology	Claimant/defendant • Making a claim (suing defendant) • Finding of liability	Prosecution/defendant • Charging defendant • Finding of guilt

However, note that in some areas the distinction between civil and criminal law can be blurred.

1   Contempt of court in a civil case may lead to a prison sentence.

2   There may be double liability (ie civil and criminal) for the same act or omission. For example, dangerous driving is a criminal offence but anyone injured by it can make a civil claim.

Key Cases Checklist

Airedale NHS Trust v Bland [1993] 1 WLR 316   HL

Key Facts

Bland was a young man who, as a result of injuries, was in a persistent vegetative state. His family wanted him to be allowed to die. They sought a declaration from the court about any medical treatment he might receive in the future. The court held that medical treatment could be withdrawn if it was in the patient's best interests.

Key Law

The duty of care owed by medical staff to a patient is limited by whether the treatment given is in the patient's best interests.

Key Judgment: Lord Goff

'. . . a doctor may, when caring for a patient who is, for example, dying of cancer, lawfully administer pain-killing drugs despite the fact that an incidental effect of that application will be to shorten the patient's life'.

2 Judicial precedent

Doctrine of precedent

- *Stare decisis*
- Like cases treated alike
- Courts bound by those above them in hierarchy
- Appellate courts normally follow own past decisions
- Only *ratio decidendi* binding
- Need good law reports

Precedent in practice

- Original precedent
- Binding precedent
- Persuasive precedent
- *Ratio* and *Obiter*
- Distinguishing
- Overruling
- Reversing

JUDICIAL PRECEDENT

Hierarchy of courts

- European Court of Justice
- Supreme Court
- Court of Appeal
- Divisional Courts
- High Court
- Inferior courts
- Overruling
- Reversing

Advantages

- Similar cases treated alike
- Certainty
- Law can develop
- Case illustrations of law

Disadvantages

- Can lead to injustice
- Too rigid
- Slow – has to wait for relevant case
- Complex – too detailed

▶ 2.1 The doctrine of precedent

2.1.1 *Stare decisis*

1   It is a fundamental principle that like cases should be treated alike.

2   The Latin maxim *stare decisis* (stand by decisions of past cases) is the basis of the doctrine of precedent.

3   Precedent, as operated in the English legal system, requires that in certain circumstances a decision on a legal point made in an earlier case MUST be followed.

4   The doctrine is that:

  ● all courts are bound to follow decisions made by courts above them in the hierarchy; and

  ● appellate courts are normally bound by their own past decisions.

5   An extreme example of this was seen following the decision in *Re Schweppes Ltd's Agreement* (1965), in which one judge in the Court of Appeal dissented. Later on the same day, when the same point of law was involved in a second case (*Re Automatic Telephone and Electric Co Ltd's Agreement* (1965)), that judge said he was now bound to follow the earlier decision.

2.1.2 Original precedent

1   Where there is no previous decision on a point of law that has to be decided by a court, then the decision made in that case on that point of law is an original precedent.

2   Usually, when faced with the situation of having to form an original precedent, the court will reason by analogy. Cases that are nearest to it in principle will be considered, though they are not binding. If there is any parallel, the court may decide that the same type of principle should apply (*Hunter and others v Canary Wharf Ltd and London Dockland Development Corporation* (1995)).

3   Such decisions used to be considered a declaratory precedent, ie the judges in the case merely declared what the law had always been, although this was the first time it had had to be decided. Supporters of this theory believed that judges did not create new law when making a decision; they merely declared what the law had always been. It is now accepted that judges do create law.

4   However, the declaratory theory still has relevance because a decision has a retrospective effect on the law (*Kleinwort Benson Ltd v Lincoln City Council* (1998)).

2.1.3 Binding and persuasive precedent

1   A past decision is binding only if:

- the legal point involved is the same as the legal point in the case now being decided;

- the facts of the present case are sufficiently similar to the previous case; and

- the earlier decision was made by a court above the present court in the hierarchy, or by a court at the same level which is bound by its own past judgments; and

- the point was argued in the case (*Kadhim v Brent London Borough Council* (2001)).

2   Only the *ratio decidendi* of the earlier case is binding (see 2.6 for details on *ratio decidendi* and *obiter dicta*).

3   A persuasive precedent is one that the court will consider and may be persuaded by, but which does not have to be followed.

4   Persuasive precedent comes from a variety of different sources. The main ones within the English legal system are:

- *obiter dicta* statements by a higher-ranking court, eg the Court of Appeal following *obiter dicta* of the House of Lords in *R v Howe* (1987) when deciding the case of *R v Gotts* (1992) on the non-availability of duress as a defence to a charge of attempted murder;

- a dissenting judgment;

- ratios from decisions by courts lower in the hierarchy.

5   Decisions by courts outside the English legal system can also have a persuasive effect on English courts. The main ones of these are:

- the Judicial Committee of the Privy Council;

- the European Court of Human Rights (s 2 Human Rights Act 1998);

- courts in other countries, especially Commonwealth countries or countries with a common law system.

2.1.4 Law reporting

For a system of precedent to operate effectively, it is essential that the reasons for decisions of past cases are properly recorded.

1   The earliest law reports were the Year Books from 1282 to 1537.

2   From 1537 to 1863, various private law reports were used. These varied in quality.

3   Since 1863 the Incorporated Council of Law Reporting has produced the official law reports.

4   There are also other well-recognised series, especially the Weekly Law Reports and the All England Law Reports.

5   Judgments of the Supreme Court and the House of Lords and some judgments of the Court of Appeal are available on official sites on the Internet.

6   Judgments from all levels of court are available on commercial subscription sites on the Internet.

7   Before the Internet, only about 70% of House of Lords cases were reported and less than a quarter of the Court of Appeal cases were reported. Unreported cases can only be cited in court with the permission of the court (*Roberts Petroleum v Bernard Kenny Ltd* (1983)).

▶ 2.2 Hierarchy of the courts

1   a) Where a point of European law is involved, the decisions of the European Court of Justice are binding on all courts in England and Wales.

    b) The European Court of Justice does not have to follow its own past decisions. This is in accordance with the more flexible approach to precedent in European countries that have civil codes.

2   a) The Supreme Court is the highest court in the UK and its decisions must be followed by all other courts in England and Wales.

    b) Although the Supreme Court replaced the House of Lords in 2009, decisions of the House of Lords prior to this are still binding on lower courts unless they have been overruled by the Supreme Court.

    c) There are exceptions to this rule where a decision conflicts with a decision of the European Court of Justice or the European Court of Human Rights.

    d) The House of Lords used to regard itself as normally bound by its own previous decisions, but would depart from a past decision where it was right to do so.

    e) The Supreme Court is not bound to follow its own past decisions. Its Practice Rules require that, if an application for permission to appeal asks the Supreme Court to depart from one of its own decisions or from one of the House of Lords, then this should be stated clearly in the application and full details must be given.

3 a) The Court of Appeal has to follow decisions of the Supreme Court/House of Lords (*Broome v Cassell & Co* (1971), *Miliangos v George Frank (Textiles) Ltd* (1976)) but see 2.5.

   b) The Court of Appeal (Civil Division) is bound to follow past decisions of its own (*Young v Bristol Aeroplane Co Ltd* (1944); see 2.5 for further detail).

   c) The Court of Appeal (Criminal Division) will normally follow its own past decisions, but has flexibility to depart from a decision where the liberty of a person is involved (*R v Taylor* (1950); see 2.5 for further detail).

4 a) Divisional courts must follow Supreme Court/House of Lords and Court of Appeal decisions.

   b) Divisional courts are normally bound by their own past decisions (*Huddersfield Police Authority v Watson* (1947)).

5 a) The High Court must follow Supreme Court/House of Lords, Court of Appeal and Divisional Court decisions.

   b) The High Court does not usually have to follow past decisions of its own. However, where there are conflicting past decisions, 'the later decision is to be preferred if it is reached after full consideration of the earlier decisions' (*Colchester Estates v Carlton Industries* (1984)).

6 Inferior courts (Crown Court, County Court, Magistrates' Court) do not create precedents and must follow decisions of all the above courts.

▶ 2.3 The House of Lords and the Practice Statement

2.3.1 The need for the Practice Statement

1 From the middle of the nineteenth century, the House of Lords generally regarded itself as bound by its own past decisions (*Beamish v Beamish* (1861)), but it was not until *London Tramways v London County Council* (1898) that this rule became completely fixed.

2 The reason for following its own past decisions was that it was in the public interest that there be certainty in the law and to prevent the same point being re-argued.

3 The ruling in *London Tramways v London County Council* had the effect of making the law too rigid.

4   In 1966 the Lord Chancellor issued the Practice Statement giving the House of Lords flexibility to depart from past decisions. The Statement said that former decisions would normally be treated as binding, but the Lords could 'depart from a previous decision when it appears right to do so'.

5   The Statement recognised that 'too rigid adherence to precedent may lead to an injustice in a particular case and also unduly restrict the proper development of the law'.

6   However, the Statement stressed the need for certainty, especially in the criminal law, and the danger of disturbing retrospectively the basis on which contracts, settlements of property and fiscal arrangements had been entered into.

2.3.2 The use of the Practice Statement

1   The Lords did not rush to use the Practice Statement. The first use was in *Conway v Rimmer* (1968), which overruled *Duncan v Cammell Laird & Co* (1942) on a technical point.

2   The first major use was in *Herrington v British Railways Board* (1972), when the House of Lords overruled (or modified) the decision in *Addie & Sons v Dumbreck* (1929) on the liability of an occupier of premises to a child trespasser.

3   However, in the same year (1972) the Lords refused to use the Practice Statement in *Jones v Secretary of State for Social Services*, even though four of the seven judges believed the earlier case of *Re Dowling* (1967) to be wrongly decided.

4   The first use of the Practice Statement in a criminal case was in *R v Shivpuri* (1986) on attempts to do the impossible, where the House of Lords overruled their previous decision of *Anderton v Ryan* (1985).

5   Since the mid-1980s, the Statement has been used a little more. For example, in civil cases it was used in:

  ● *Murphy v Brentwood District Council* (1991) to overrule the decision in *Anns v London Borough of Merton* (1978);

  ● *Pepper v Hart* (1993) to overrule *Davis v Johnson* (1979) on the use of Hansard as an extrinsic aid to interpretation.

In criminal cases it has been used in:

  ● *R v Howe* (1987) to overrule *DPP for Northern Ireland v Lynch* (1975) on the availability of the defence of duress to a murdr charge;

- *R v Adomako* (1994), which overruled *R v Seymour* (1983) on the test for recklessness in manslaughter;

- *R v G and R* (2003), which overruled *Caldwell* (1982) on objective recklessness in criminal damage.

6   However, there are also many examples of refusal to use the Practice Statement. See, for example:

- *Jones v Secretary of State for Social Services* (1972);

- *R v Kansal* (*No 2*) (2001) on whether the Human Rights Act 1998 was retrospective.

▶ 2.4 The Supreme Court

1   In October 2009, the House of Lords was abolished and replaced by the Supreme Court.

2   The Practice Direction applied to the House of Lords and, strictly speaking, does not apply to the Supreme Court.

3   The Practice Rules of the Supreme Court state that 'If an application for permission to appeal asks the Supreme Court to depart from one of its own decisions or from one of the House of Lords', this should be stated clearly in the application and full details must be given.

4   Also in *Austin v London Borough of Southwark* (2010) The Supreme Court confirmed that the power to use the Practice Statement had been transferred to them, although they did not use the Practice Statement in that case.

5   This shows that the Supreme Court is prepared to depart from previous decisions. However, it seems likely that the court will only do so where there is a very good reason to do so.

▶ 2.5 The position of the Court of Appeal

Must follow decisions of the Supreme Court/
House of Lords (*Broome v Cassell, Miliangos*).

Possible exceptions where a Supreme Court/
House of Lords' decision:
- has been overruled by the European Court of
  Justice; or
- is incompatible with the European Convention
  on Human Rights.

COURT OF APPEAL

CIVIL DIVISION

Must follow own past
decisions (*Davis v Johnson*).

Exceptions in *Young's* case:
- conflicting decisions;
- impliedly overruled by
- House of Lords;
- *per incuriam*.

CRIMINAL DIVISION

Normally follows own past
decisions.

Same exceptions in *Young's*
case apply.

Also will not follow where
law has been misapplied or
misunderstood (*Gould*).

1   The Court of Appeal is bound to follow decisions of the European Court
    of Justice and the Supreme Court/House of Lords.

2   In the 1970s, there was a challenge (mainly by Lord Denning) to the
    rule that the Court of Appeal must follow House of Lords' decisions.

3   In *Broome v Cassell & Co* (1971), the Court of Appeal refused to
    follow *Rookes v Barnard* (1964) on the circumstances in which exem-
    plary damages could be awarded. When *Broome v Cassell* was appealed
    to the House of Lords, the Law Lords reminded the Court of Appeal that
    it was 'necessary for each lower tier, including the Court of Appeal, to
    accept loyally the decisions of the higher tiers'.

4   In the cases of *Schorsch Meier GmbH v Hennin* (1975) and *Miliangos
    v George Frank (Textiles) Ltd* (1975), the Court of Appeal refused to
    follow the House of Lords' decision in *Havana Railways* (1961) that
    damages could only be awarded in sterling. On the appeal of *Miliangos* to

the House of Lords, the judges stated that 'the Court of Appeal is absolutely bound by a decision of the House of Lords'.

5 Since *Miliangos*, there has been no further challenge to this basic principle of judicial precedent, except where:

- a decision of the House of Lords is not compatible with the European Convention on Human Rights (*Director General of Fair Trading v The Proprietary Association of Great Britain* (2001), *Ghaidan v Godin-Mendoza* (2002));

- a decision of the House of Lords has been subsequently overruled by the European Court of Justice.

6 In *R v James: R v Karimi* (2006), the Court of Appeal refused to follow a decision of the House of Lords on the law of provocation as a defence to murder. Instead, they followed a decision of the Judicial Committee of the Privy Council. This was mainly because the panel of judges making the decision in Holley comprised nine Law Lords.

2.5.1 Court of Appeal (Civil Division) and its own past decisions

1 The divisions do not bind each other.

2 The Civil Division must follow its own past decisions, unless they come within the exceptions in *Young v Bristol Aeroplane Co Ltd* (1944).

3 These exceptions are:

- the court is entitled to decide which of two conflicting past decisions of its own it will follow;

- the court must refuse to follow a decision of its own which, though not expressly overruled, cannot stand with a decision of the House of Lords (now Supreme Court);

- the court is not bound to follow a decision of its own if it is satisfied that the decision was given *per incuriam*.

4 There is possibly another exception in interlocutory cases where an earlier decision made by a two-judge court can be overruled by a later three-judge court (*Boys v Chaplin* (1968)).

5 After 1966, Lord Denning argued that the principle of the Practice Statement should apply to the Court of Appeal, so that it would not be bound by its own past decisions. His main ground for arguing this for the Court of Appeal was that it was effectively the last appellate court in the vast majority of cases.

6   In *Davis v Johnson* (1979), the Court of Appeal refused to follow a past decision of its own made only a few days earlier. However, on appeal to the House of Lords, the Law Lords 'unequivocally and unanimously' re-affirmed the rule in *Young v Bristol Aeroplane*.

7   Since *Davis v Johnson* there has been no challenge by the Court of Appeal to the rule in *Young v Bristol Aeroplane*.

8   However, the Court of Appeal has used the *per incuriam* exception on some occasions (*Williams v Fawcett* (1985), *Rickards v Rickards* (1989), *Rakhit v Carty* (1990)).

2.5.2 Court of Appeal (Criminal Division) and its own past decisions

1   a) In *R v Taylor* (1950), the Court of Criminal Appeal (the predecessor of the Court of Appeal (Criminal Division)) took the view that the exceptions that applied in civil cases 'ought not to be the only ones applied' in criminal cases.

    b) The court held that as the liberty of the subject was involved, an earlier decision should not be followed where law has been misapplied or misunderstood.

2   In *R v Gould* (1968), the newly created Court of Appeal (Criminal Division) held that this same flexibility still applied.

3   In *R v Spencer* (1985), the Criminal Division stated that there was no difference between it and the Civil Division in respect of being bound by past decisions, save that when the liberty of the subject is at stake it might decline to follow one of its own decisions.

4   Where there are conflicting past decisions, the Criminal Division will prefer the one that favours the defendant (*R v Jenkins* (1983)).

▶ 2.6 *Ratio* and *obiter*

1   In a judgment, there are several elements. There will always be:

● findings of material facts;

● statements of the principles of law;

● the decision based on these two.

2   Only the principles of law that are essential to the decision are the *ratio decidendi*.

3   Statements of principles of law that are not relevant to the decision are *obiter dicta*.

4   Cross defines *ratio decidendi* as 'any rule expressly or impliedly treated by the judge as a necessary step in reaching his conclusion'.

5   Zander defines *ratio decidendi* as 'a proposition of law which decides the case, in the light or in the context of the material facts'.

6   Discovering the *ratio decidendi* of a case is not always easy, for many reasons:

   ● it is hardly ever stated expressly;

   ● in appellate courts there may be more than one judgment with different ratios;

   ● in extreme cases, it may even be impossible to find the ratio (*Central Asbestos Co Ltd v Dodd* (1973)).

7   Although the ratio is given in the judgment of the first case, it is to a great extent determined by the court in a later case. It may be enlarged by being applied to a wider situation, or restricted by being confined to a narrow scope.

8   *Obiter dicta* can be persuasive (*High Trees* case (1947)).

▶ 2.7 Distinguishing

1   Where a judge considers that the material facts of the present case are sufficiently different from an earlier case, they are distinguishing the case and may refuse to follow the earlier decision (*Merritt v Merritt* (1970), *Balfour v Balfour* (1919)).

2   Distinguishing is a major factor in allowing the doctrine of precedent to remain flexible.

3   Decisions that are questionable or unpopular may be restricted to a narrow area by distinguishing.

▶ 2.8 Advantages and disadvantages of precedent

It is important to realise that for nearly all the factors that can be given as an advantage, there is also a disadvantage.

2.8.1 Advantages

1   It serves the interests of justice and fairness, as similar cases are seen to be treated in a similar way.

2   It creates certainty in the law and allows lawyers to advise clients on the probable outcome of a case.

3   There is opportunity for the law to develop and change with society (*Herrington v British Railways Board* (1972)).

4   As decisions are based on real cases, there are practical illustrations of the law.

5   It is a time-saving device, as for most situations there is an existing solution.

2.8.2 Disadvantages

1   The doctrine as applied in the English legal system is too rigid. This mainly stems from two factors:

● the House of Lords was reluctant to use the Practice Statement, but the Supreme Court may be more flexible; and

● the Court of Appeal is bound to follow decisions of the Supreme Court/House of Lords.

2   This rigidity can create injustice in an individual case.

3   The law is slow to develop; it is recognised that areas of law are unclear and in need of reform, but changes cannot be made unless a case on the particular point of law comes before the court.

4   The law is complex, with too many fine distinctions.

5   The large number of reported cases make it difficult to find the relevant law.

▶ 2.9 Judicial law-making in precedent

1   Large areas of law have been developed by the judges, for example rules on formation of contracts, the tort of negligence and the meaning of 'intention' in criminal law.

2   The right of judges to create and/or reform law is unconstitutional, as judges are not our elected law-makers.

3   The development of the law can depend on whether the judge is an active or passive law-maker.

4   Active law-making can be seen in R v R (1991), where the House of Lords ruled that there was a crime of marital rape.

5   Passive law-making is illustrated by C v DPP (1995), where the House of Lords refused to change a common law presumption about the criminal responsibility of children under the age of 14, stating that it was for Parliament to make such changes.

Key Cases Checklist

Binding Effect

Automatic Telephone and Electric Co Ltd v Registrar of Restrictive Trading Agreements (1965)
A judgment has immediately binding effect on lower courts and on appellate courts of the same standing

Kleinwort Benson Ltd v Lincoln City Council (1998)
An overruled case is regarded as never having been law

Court Hierarchy

Broome v Cassell & Co (1971)
Decisions by higher courts are binding on all lower courts

Miliangos v George Frank (Textiles) Ltd (1975)
The Court of Appeal must follow decisions of the House of Lords (now the Supreme Court)

Judicial precedent (1)

The House of Lords (now the Supreme Court

Practice Statement [Judicial Precedent] (1966)
The House of Lords was normally bound by their own past decisions but could depart from them where 'it appeared right to do so'

Herrington v British Railways Board (1972)
First use of Practice Statement in mainstream area of law

R v Shivpuri (1986)
First use of Practice Statement in criminal case

R v G and R (2003)
Use of Practice Statement to overrule major decision on the meaning of recklessness

2.1.1

Schweppes Ltd v Registrar of Restrictive Trading Agreements [1965] 1 All ER 195 and *Automatic Telephone and Electric Co Ltd v Registrar of Restrictive Trading Agreements* [1965] 1 All ER 206

 CA

Key Facts

Both cases involved the same point of law on discovery of documents in restrictive trade practices. In the *Schweppes* case, Willmer LJ dissented with the majority decision. The *Automatic Telephone* case was heard by the same three judges later the same day. In this case, Willmer LJ accepted that he was now bound by precedent and agreed with the decision of the other two judges.

Key Law

A judgment has immediate binding effect on an appellate court of the same standing (and also on any lower court).

Key Judgment: Willmer LJ

'It seems to me, however, that I am now bound by the decision of the majority in the previous case. In these circumstances I have no alternative but to concur in saying that the appeal in the present case should be allowed.'

2.1.2

Kleinwort Benson Ltd v Lincoln City Council [1998] 4 All ER 513

 HL

Key Facts

A financial arrangement known as 'interest rate swap trans-action' was held to be unlawful by the Court of Appeal in 1991. Many local authorities had entered into such an arrangement prior to this date. A claim was made by the bank for the return of the money given to the council under the arrangement on the basis that the money had been paid under a mistake of law. An earlier Court of Appeal case had held that money paid under a mistake of law was not recoverable. The House of Lords ruled in *Kleinwort* that the bank could rely on the mistake of law, even though, at the time the agreement was made, it was legal under the law as it was thought to be at time.

Key Law

When a point of law is decided by overruling an earlier case, the overruled case is regarded as never having been the law and it is not applied in later cases or the instant case. This is so even though the agreement that is the subject of the claim was made before the earlier case was overruled.

Key Judgment: Lord Browne-Wilkinson

'The theoretical position has been that judges do not make or change law: they discover and declare the law which is throughout the same. According to this theory, when an earlier decision is overruled the law is not changed: its true nature is disclosed, having existed in that form all along. This theoretical position is, as Lord Reid said, a fairy tale in which no longer anyone believes. In truth, judges make and change the law. The whole of the common law is judge-made and only by judicial change in the law is the common law kept relevant in a changing world.'

Key Comment

Although the declaratory theory is no longer regarded as the position, precedent still has a retrospective effect. This can lead to the unjust situation that parties in the instant case will have relied on the law as it was at the time of the making of the agreement, only to be told that it is not the law and never has been.

1.2

Broome v Cassell & Co [1971] 2 All ER 187 CA, [1972] 1 All ER 801 HL

Key Facts

The Court of Appeal held that the House of Lords' decision in *Rookes v Barnard* (1964) on the circumstances in which exemplary damages could be awarded was wrong. The Court of Appeal pointed out that the House of Lords had ignored earlier decisions in *Hulton & Co v Jones* (1910) and *Ley v Hamilton* (1935). When *Broome v Cassell* was appealed to the House of Lords, they held that the Court of Appeal was bound to follow decisions of the House of Lords.

Key Law

Decisions by higher courts are binding on all lower courts.

Key Judgment: Lord Hailsham

'It is not open to the Court of Appeal to give advice to the judges of first instance to ignore decisions of the House of Lords . . . The fact is, and I hope it will never be necessary to say so again, that, in the hierarchical system of courts which exists in this country, it is necessary for each lower tier, including the Court of Appeal, to accept loyally the decisions of the higher tiers.'

N.B. This now also applies to Supreme Court decisions.

2.5

Miliangos v George Frank (Textiles) Ltd [1975] 1 All ER 1076 CA, [1975] 3 All ER 801 HL

Key Facts

The claimant, M. who was a Swiss national, supplied yarn to an English company under a contract which provided for payment to be made in Swiss francs. The company failed to pay and M made a claim in the English courts. He asked that the award be in Swiss francs and not in English pounds as the value of the pound had fallen. There was a House of Lords decision, *Re United Railways of Havana* (1960), which stated that judgments could only be given in pounds and not in any other currency. The Court of Appeal in *Schorsch Meier GmbH v Hennin* (1975) had refused to follow this decision of the House of Lords. The House of Lords held that the change in the stability of the pound was a good reason to depart from their earlier decision, but they also pointed out that the Court of Appeal had no right to do this.

Key Law

(1) The House of Lords had power under the Practice Statement to overrule its own past decisions.

(2) Lower courts are bound to follow decisions of higher courts.

Key Judgment: Lord Simon

'Courts which are bound by the rule of precedent are not free to disregard an otherwise binding precedent on the ground that the reason which led to the formulation of the rule embodied in such precedent seems to the court to have lost cogency.'

Key Comment

It seems likely that if the Court of Appeal, in *Schorsch Meier GmbH v Hennin*, had not departed from the decision of the House of Lords in *Re United Railways of Havana*, then the case of *Miliangos* may never have been appealed to the House of Lords. This would have meant that the House of Lords did not have the opportunity to review its earlier decision

Practice Statement [Judicial Precedent] [1966] 3 All ER 77

Key Facts

'Their Lordships regard the use of precedent as an indispensable foundation upon which to decide what is the law and its application to individual cases. It provides at least some degree of certainty upon which individuals can rely in the conduct of their affairs, as well as a basis for orderly development of legal rules.

Their Lordships nevertheless recognise that the rigid adherence to precedent may lead to injustice in a particular case and also unduly restrict the proper development of the law. They, therefore, propose to modify their present practice and while treating former decisions of this House as normally binding, to depart from a previous decision when it appears right to do so.

In this connection they will bear in mind the danger of disturbing retrospectively the basis on which contracts, settlement of property and fiscal arrangements have been entered into and also the especial need for certainty as to the criminal law.

This announcement is not intended to affect the use of precedent elsewhere than in this House.'

N.B. Although this does not technically apply to the Supreme Court, that court is also prepared to overrule its own past decisions.

2.3.2

Herrington v British Railways Board [1972] AC 877

Key Facts

A 6-year-old boy was badly burned when playing on a railway track. The Railway Board knew that the fence alongside the railway line was damaged and that children had been seen playing on the track for some weeks before the boy was injured. A previous decision of the House of Lords in *Robert Addie & Sons (Collieries Ltd) v Dumbreck* (1929) had ruled that an occupier did not owe a duty of care to a trespasser. The House of Lords relied on the Practice Statement to over-rule the *Robert Addie* case and to restate the law on the extent of duty of care owed by an occupier to a trespasser.

Key Law

The Practice Statement could be used to overrule old cases where social attitudes had changed.

2.3.2

R v Shivpuri [1986] 2 All ER 334

Key Facts

D thought he was dealing in prohibited drugs. In fact it was snuff and harmless vegetable matter. In an earlier case, *Anderton v Ryan* (1985), the House of Lords had held that there could not be an attempt in this sort of situation. However, in Shivpuri, they accepted that their decision in *Anderton v Ryan* had been wrong and used the Practice Statement to overrule it, even though that case had been decided only a year earlier.

Key Law

Even though the Practice Statement stressed need for 'especial certainty as to the criminal law', the House of Lords could use it to overrule an earlier case in the criminal law as well as in civil law.

Key Judgment: Lord Bridge

'I am undeterred by the consideration that the decision in *Anderton v Ryan* was so recent. The 1966 Practice

Statement is an effective abandonment of our pretention to infallibility. If a serious error embodied in a decision of this House has distorted the law, the sooner it is corrected the better.'

2.3.2   *R v G and R* [2003] UKHL 50   HL

Key Facts
....

The defendants were two boys, aged 11 and 12 years. They set fire to some bundles of newspapers which they threw under a large wheelie bin in a shop yard. The bin caught fire and this spread to the shop and other buildings causing about £1 million damage. The boys were convicted under both s 1 and s 3 of the Criminal Damage Act 1971 on the basis of objective recklessness (i.e. that an ordinary adult would have realised the risk). On appeal the House of Lords quashed their conviction and overruled the decision in *Metropolitan Police Commissioner v Caldwell* (1981), holding that the Law Lords in that case had 'adopted an interpretation of section 1 of the 1971 Act which was beyond the range of feasible meanings'.

Key Law
....

The House of Lords was entitled to use the Practice Statement to overrule previous decisions.

Following House of Lords / Supreme Court

***Miliangos v George Frank (Textiles) Ltd* (1975)**
The Court of Appeal must follow decisions of the House of Lords/Supreme Court

***Mendoza v Ghaidan* (2002)**
The Court of Appeal may take into account European Court of Human Rights decisions in preference

Own past decisions

***Young v Bristol Aeroplane Co Ltd* (1944)**
Court of Appeal is normally bound by its own past decisions

There are 3 exceptions:
- conflicting past decisions
- decision of House of Lords/Supreme Court which effectively overrules CA decision
- *per incuriam*

***Davis v Johnson* (1978)**
The Court of Appeal must follow its own past decisions unless one of the exceptions in *Young's case* applies

**Judicial precedent (2)
Court of Appeal**

Per incuriam

***Williams v Fawcett* (1985)**
Refused to follow earlier decisions as they were based on error

***Rickards v Rickards* (1989)**
Refused to follow earlier decision where the effect of a statute had been overlooked

The *per incuriam* power should only be used in 'rare and exceptional cases'

Criminal division

***R v Gould* (1968)**
Criminal Division of the Court of Appeal does not have to follow precedent as rigidly as the Civil Division

***R v Spencer* (1986)**
Criminal Division is subject to the same rules as the Civil Division except that it may refuse to follow precedent where liberty is at stake

---

2.5   *Schorsch Meier GmbH v Hennin* [1975] 1 All ER 152   (CA)

Key Facts

The court had to consider whether damages had to be awarded in sterling or whether they could be in another currency. There was a decision by the House of Lords in the *Havana Railway* case (1960) that damages had to be in sterling. The Court of Appeal refused to follow this because sterling was no longer a stable currency. Justice required that damages be awarded in German marks otherwise the claimant would not have received the true value of his claim.

Key Law

See next case.

2.5

Miliangos v George Frank [Textiles] Ltd **[1975] 1 All ER 1076, CA, [1975] 3 All ER 801**   HL

Key Facts

See 1.2.

Key Law

The Court of Appeal is bound to follow decisions of the House of Lords and the Supreme Court.

Key Link

Broome v Cassell & Co [1971] 2 All ER 187 CA, [1972] 1 All ER 801 HL (see 1.2).

2.5

Mendoza v Ghaidan **[2002] EWCA Civ 1533**   CA

Key Facts

The Court of Appeal (Civil Division) 'revisited' the House of Lords' decision in *Fitzpatrick v Sterling Housing Association* (2001) on the application of the Rent Act 1977. They did this because s 2 of the Human Rights Act 1998 requires courts to 'take into account' decisions of the European Court of Human Rights.

Key Law

Where there is a human rights issue, the Court of Appeal (and all other courts) must take into account decisions of the European Court of Human Rights. This can lead to the Court of Appeal following of the European Court of Human Rights in preference to a decision of the Supreme Court or the House of Lords.

Key Link

The Court of Appeal also preferred a decision by the European Court of Human Rights to that of the House of Lords in *Director General of Fair Trading v The Proprietary Association of Great Britain* (2001).

2.2

Young v Bristol Aeroplane Co Ltd [1944] 2 All ER 293

Key Facts

A workman, who had already received compensation under the Workman's Compensation Acts for injuries suffered at work, claimed damages from his employer. The defence argued that an earlier decision of the Court of Appeal prevented a claim for damages where statutory compensation had been received. It was held that the Court of Appeal had to follow its own past decisions.

Key Law

The Court of Appeal (Civil Division) is normally bound by its own previous decisions. However, *Young's case* set out three exceptions to this rule:

● where there are conflicting decisions in past Court of Appeal cases, the court can choose which one it will follow and which it will reject;

● where there is a decision of the House of Lords which effectively overrules a Court of Appeal decision the Court of Appeal must follow the decision of the House of Lords (now the Supreme Court);

● where the decision was made *per incuriam*, that is carelessly or by mistake because a relevant Act of Parliament or other regulation has not been considered by the court.

Key Judgment: Lord Greene MR

'We have come to the clear conclusion that this court is bound to follow previous decisions of its own . . . The only exceptions to this rule . . . we here summarise: (1) The court is entitled and bound to decide which of two conflicting decisions of its own it will follow. (2) The court is bound to refuse to follow a decision of its own which, though not expressly overruled, cannot, in its opinion, stand with a decision of the House of Lords. (3) The court is not bound to follow a decision of its own if it is satisfied that the decision was given *per incuriam*.'

2.5.1

Davis v Johnson [1978] 1 All ER 1132 (HL)

Key Facts

A young unmarried mother applied for an injunction ordering her violent partner to leave their flat. The tenancy of the flat was in their joint names. Earlier cases in the Court of Appeal had held that an injunction could not be granted where the partner had a right in the property (in this case a tenancy). The Court of Appeal refused to follow its earlier decisions. On appeal to the House of Lords, it was held that the earlier cases had been wrongly decided, but the House of Lords reminded the Court of Appeal that they were bound to follow its own previous decisions, subject to the exceptions in *Young's case*.

Key Law

The Court of Appeal is bound to follow its own previous decisions, subject to the exceptions in *Young's case*.

Key Judgment: House of Lords, Lord Diplock

'In an appellate court of last resort a balance must be struck between the need on the one hand for the legal certainty resulting from the binding effect of previous decisions and, on the other side, the avoidance of undue restriction on the proper development of the law. In the case of an intermediate appellate court, however, the second desideratum can be taken care of by appeal to a superior appellate court, if reasonable means of access to it are available; while the risk to the first desideratum, legal certainty, if the court is not bound by its own previous decisions grows ever greater. So the balance does not lie in the same place as a court of last resort.'

Key Comment

The judgments in this case demonstrate the arguments for and against the Court of Appeal having more freedom to depart from its own previous decisions. It is noticeable that since this case, the Court of Appeal has always followed the decisions of the House of Lords and the Supreme Court, except where there has been a decision of the European Court of Justice, the European Court of Human Rights (or in one exceptional case, the Privy Council – see *R v James*: *R v Karimi* (2006)).

2.5.1   *Williams v Fawcett* [1985] 1 All ER 787   CA

Key Facts

The issue was about the formalities necessary for a notice to commit someone for contempt. There had been four previous Court of Appeal decisions on the point. The court refused to follow these earlier decisions on the ground that they were based on error.

 ### Key Law

The Court of Appeal is not bound to follow a previous decision of its own if that decision was reached *per incuriam*.

 2.5.1   *Rickards v Rickards* [1989] 3 All ER 193   CA

Key Facts

An ex-husband failed to appeal within the time limits following a financial order in divorce proceedings. His later application for an extension of time to appeal was refused. He appealed to the Court of Appeal. There were previous decisions of the court holding that it had no authority to hear such an appeal. There was, however, a statutory provision to the contrary. The Court of Appeal, therefore, refused to follow its previous decisions and held that it could hear the appeal.

Key Law

The Court of Appeal can refuse to follow a previous decision of its own, if that decision was made in error where the effect of an earlier decision has been misunderstood. This power should only be used in 'rare and exceptional cases'.

 ### Key Judgment: Lord Donaldson

'This court is justified in refusing to follow one of its own previous decisions not only where that decision is given in ignorance or forgetfulness of some statutory provision or some authority binding upon it, but also, in rare and exceptional cases, if it is satisfied that the decision involved a manifest slip or error.'

Key Comment

This case was considered to be 'rare and exceptional' because:

(a) a wrongful denial of jurisdiction was a serious matter amounting to breach of a statutory duty on the part of the Court of Appeal; and

(b) it was most unlikely (because of the cost involved) that the House of Lords would be presented with an opportunity to correct the mistake.

Key Link

Rakhit v Carty [1990] 2 All ER 202.

2.5.2   *R v Gould* [1968] 1 All ER 849

Key Facts

D was convicted of bigamy. The issue was whether an honest and reasonable belief that, at the date of the second marriage, the first marriage had been dissolved, was a good defence. The earlier case of *R v Wheat: R v Stocks* (1921) had ruled that such a mistake was not a good defence. The court held that it was not bound to follow its own previous decision and quashed the conviction.

Key Law

In cases which involve the liberty of the subject, the Criminal Division of the Court of Appeal does not have to apply the doctrine of precedent as rigidly as the Civil Division.

Key Judgment: Diplock LJ

'In its criminal jurisdiction which it has inherited from the Court of Criminal Appeal, the Court of Appeal does not apply the doctrine of *stare decisis* with the same rigidity as in its civil jurisdiction. If on due consideration we were to be of the opinion that the law had been either misapplied or misunderstood in an earlier decision of this court, or its predecessor the Court of Criminal Appeal, we should be entitled to depart from the view as to the law expressed in the earlier decision notwithstanding that the case could not be brought within any of the exceptions laid down in *Young v Bristol Aeroplane Co Ltd*.'

2.5.2

R v Spencer [1985] 1 All ER 673 CA, [1986] 2 All ER 928 HL

 CA

Key Facts

The issue before the court was whether the Court of Appeal (Criminal Division) was bound by a previous decision of its own.

Key Law

The Criminal Division of the Court of Appeal is subject to the same rules of precedent as the Civil Division, save that when the liberty of the subject is at stake, it may decline to follow one of its own previous decisions.

The Privy Council

R v James: R v Karimi (2006)
Where there are conflicting decisions of the House of Lords or Supreme Court and Privy Council, English courts should normally follow the decision of the House of Lords or Supreme Court. In the exceptional circumstances of this case the decision of the Privy Council would be followed

Judicial precedent (3)

Distinguishing

Merritt v Merritt (1970)
The parties had agreed to separate, so the case could be distinguished from:

Balfour v Balfour (1919)
where the wife was unable to go with husband because she was ill

Judicial law-making

Donoghue v Stevenson (1932)
The tort of negligence was developed by judicial decision

R v R (1991)
Judges ruled that marital rape was a criminal offence

C v DPP (1995)
Judges refused to change the law on the presumption that children under 14 were *doli incapax*

2.5

R v James: R v Karimi [2006] EWCA Crim 14 CA

Key Facts

In both cases D was charged with murder. At both trials the judge had directed the jury that the law on provocation was stated by the Judicial Committee of the Privy Council in *A-G for Jersey v Holley* (2005) rather than as stated by the House of Lords in *Smith (Morgan)* (2001). D appealed on the ground that the House of Lords decision was the one that governed English law. The Court of Appeal held that in the exceptional circumstances of *A-G for Jersey v Holley* the decision of the Privy Council was to be preferred.

Key Law

Where there is conflict between decisions of the House of Lords or Supreme Court and the Judicial Committee of the Privy Council, the normal rule is that courts in the English legal system are bound by the House of Lords' or Supreme Court's decision. However, in exceptional circumstances, courts may follow the Privy Council.

Key Comment

The case of *Holley* was exceptional in that nine of the twelve Law Lords formed the panel for the case and the decision was reached on a majority of six to three. The judges stated in their judgments that the result reached by the majority clarified definitively the English law.

2.7

Balfour v Balfour [1919] 2 KB 571 CA

Key Facts

A husband had to go abroad to work but his wife was unable to go with him because of illness. The husband agreed that he would pay his wife an allowance of £30 per month. He failed to pay the allowance and the wife sued him for breach of contract. The action failed as there was no intention to create legal relations. There was merely a domestic arrangement.

Compare this to the next case.

2.7

Merritt v Merritt [1970] 1 WLR 1211

Key Facts

A husband had deserted his wife for another woman. He and his wife came to an agreement that the husband would pay her £40 per month: the wife would pay the mortgage on their house and, when the mortgage was paid off, the husband would transfer his share of the house to her. This part of the agreement was written down. The husband later refused to transfer the house. The wife claimed for breach of contract. The court held there was an enforceable contract and that the husband was in breach of contract.

Key Law

The court distinguished the second case from the first case on the facts. In *Balfour*, although the parties were living apart, they were not separated. Their arrangement was purely a domestic matter. In *Merritt*, the parties had separated and, following this, they had made an agreement part of which was in writing. Although they were still husband and wife, their agreement was clearly meant as a legally enforceable contract.

2.9

R v R (Rape: Marital Exemption) [1991] 4 All ER 481

Key Facts

D and his wife had separated and agreed to seek a divorce. Three weeks later D broke into the wife's parents' home, where she was staying, and attempted to rape her.

Key Law

Although old authorities stated that a man could not be guilty of raping his wife, the law had to evolve to suit modern society. D could be guilty.

Key Judgment: Lord Keith of Kinkel

'[The] question is whether . . . this is an area where the court should step aside to leave the matter to the parliamentary process. This is not the creation of a new offence, it is the removal of a common law fiction which has become anachronistic and offensive and we consider that it is our duty, having reached that conclusion, to act upon it.'

Key Comment

D took the case to the European Court of Human Rights claiming that the retrospective recognition of marital rape was a breach of Art 7 of the European Convention on Human Rights. Marital rape was not a crime at the time D committed the act, but he was still found guilty of the offence. It was held that there was no breach of Art 7. In fact, abandoning the idea that a husband could not be prosecuted for rape of his wife, conformed to one of the fundamental objectives of the Convention, that of respect for human dignity.

2.9   *C v DPP* [1995] 2 All ER 43   HL

Key Facts

A 12-year-old boy was charged with interfering with a motor vehicle with intent to commit theft. The defence relied on the common law presumption of *doli incapax* which meant that a child aged between 10 and 14 could not be convicted unless the prosecution proved that he knew that his act was seriously wrong. He was convicted. On appeal to the Divisional court it was held that the *doli incapax* presumption was outdated and no longer good law. The case was then appealed to the House of Lords who allowed the appeal. They held that the presumption was still part of English law and that the courts did not have the right to abolish it.

Key Law

Where the issue is not a purely legal one, then law making should be left to Parliament.

3 Legislation

Acts of Parliament

- Pressure for legislation
- Consultation
- Green and White Papers
- Drafting process
- Passage through Parliament
- Coming into force

LEGISLATION

Delegated legislation

- Types
  - a) Orders in Council
  - b) Statutory instruments
  - c) By-laws
- Need for delegated legislation
- Control by Parliament
- Control by the courts

▶ 3.1 Acts of Parliament

About 70 to 80 Acts of Parliament are passed each year. In addition there is a considerable amount of delegated legislation each year, including over 3,000 statutory instruments. If a legislative provision is not clear then the judges have to interpret it in order to apply it.

3.1.1 Pre-parliamentary process and consultation

1   Pressure for new laws comes from a variety of sources. The main ones are:

- Government policy;
- EU Law;
- Law Commission reports;
- reports by other commissions or committees;
- pressure groups.

2   The Government sets out its legislative programme for the parliamentary session in the Queen's Speech at the opening of Parliament.

3   Usually the government department responsible for the projected legislation will decide whether to consult prior to issuing a Green Paper.

4   *Making the Law* (1992), a Report by the Hansard Society, emphasised the need for consultation. It pointed out that the lack of consultation could lead to last-minute changes in Bills as they went through Parliament, as happened with the Broadcasting Bill 1989.

5   Consultation has become more common in recent years.

6   The Law Commission has a duty to review areas of law and will research and consult before drawing up proposals for reform.

7   Some Bills may be the result of reports by other committees or commissions, which will have heard evidence about the issues concerned.

3.1.2 Green and White Papers

1   A Green Paper sets out the tentative proposals for changes to the law and invites comments.

2   Green Papers were first used in 1967 and are now usually used as part of the legislative process.

3   A White Paper is a firm proposal for a new law. Sometimes there may be a draft Bill annexed to the White Paper.

3.1.3 The drafting process

1   A draft Act is called a Bill.

2   The vast majority of Bills are introduced by the Government of the day. These Government Bills are drafted by parliamentary counsel to the Treasury.

3   The government department responsible for the legislation will give detailed instructions to the parliamentary counsel.

4   The Renton Committee, in *Preparation of Legislation* (1975), criticised the quality of draftsmanship. The four main criticisms were:

   ● the language used in statutes was obscure and complex;

   ● over-elaboration in an effort to obtain certainty;

   ● illogical and unhelpful structure;

   ● amendment of previous Acts by later Acts making it difficult to discover the current law.

5   Since 1998 there must be a written statement that the Bill is compatible with the European Convention on Human Rights. Alternatively, the Government can say that no such statement could be made but that it wishes to proceed with the Bill.

▌ 3.2 The process in Parliament

Each Bill goes through a number of stages before it becomes an Act. If the Bill is voted against at the Second Reading or Third Reading in either House then it does not become law.

3.2.1 Introducing a Bill to Parliament

1   Bills can be introduced into Parliament in the House of Commons or the House of Lords.

2   Government Bills are introduced by the Government through the relevant minister; such Bills are known as Government Bills and will almost always become law as the Government usually has a majority in the House of Commons.

3   A Private Member's Bill is one which is introduced by a backbench MP. There are three ways in which this can be done:

   ● drawing a position in the ballot held in each Parliamentary session;

   ● under Standing Order No 39;

   ● under the ten-minute rule (Standing Order No 10).

4   The time in Parliament for Private Members' Bills is very limited. Unless the Bill is supported by the Government it only has a small chance of becoming law.

3.2.2 Types of Bill

1   Public Bill – one which relates to matters that affect the general public; most Government Bills will be Public Bills.

2   Private Bill – one which relates to the powers and interests of certain private individuals or institutions (eg University College London Act 1996). The procedure for a Private Bill is slightly different to that for a Public Bill, with the Committee stage being the most important aspect, while the Second and Third Readings are more of a formality.

3   Hybrid Bill – one with features of both a Public and a Private Bill (eg Channel Tunnel Bill 1986–87).

3.2.3 Passing a Bill

A Bill may be started in either the House of Commons or the House of Lords, but it has to go through the same procedure in each House and pass all stages of the legislative process in order to become law.

1   First Reading – a formality at which the title of the Bill is read out and a day named for the Second Reading.

2   Second Reading – the main debate on the principles of the Bill.

3   Committee Stage – a consideration of each clause of the Bill.

4   Report Stage – a report to the whole House of amendments proposed by the Committee stage.

5   Third Reading – the final vote on the Bill; there will be a further debate about the Bill only if at least six members request it.

6   The other house – if the Bill started in the House of Commons, then the above five stages are carried out in the House of Lords, and vice versa.

7   Royal Assent – a formal assent to the Bill by the Monarch. The Bill is now an Act of Parliament.

3.2.4 The Parliament Acts 1911 and 1949

1   The House of Lords' power to prevent Bills from becoming law is limited by these Acts.

2   For a 'Money Bill' that has been passed by the House of Commons, the Government may choose to re-introduce that Bill after one month and, if it passes the House of Commons for a second time, it then becomes law.

3   For all other Bills the delay time is one year.

4   The House of Commons very rarely uses the power under the Parliament Acts (eg War Crimes Act 1991, Hunting Act 2004).

5   Where a Bill has been started in the House of Lords but has been voted against, it cannot be re-introduced.

3.2.5 Coming into force

1   An Act of Parliament comes into force on:

- the commencement date (if any) given in the Act; or
- the date set by the appropriate Government Minister if there is an 'appointed day' section; or
- midnight following the Royal Assent if there is no indication in the Act.

2   There is much criticism of the use of appointed day sections, where different parts of the Act may be brought into effect at different times. This makes it difficult to discover whether a certain provision is in force or not.

3   Some sections may never be brought into force, bringing into question why they were enacted in the first place.

▶ 3.3 Advantages of statute law over case law

1   There is the opportunity for consultation.

2   Law can be passed to avoid future problems.

3   The change to the law is usually prospective, thus not affecting existing contracts, etc. However, a few Acts have been made retrospective (War Damage Act 1965, War Crimes Act 1991).

4   The law is known in advance, rather than after the judgment in a case.

5   An Act can cover a wide range of points.

6   Statutory law supersedes common law.

7   It cannot normally be challenged because of the sovereignty of Parliament.

▶ 3.4 Parliamentary sovereignty

1   No challenge can normally be made to an Act of Parliament.

2   This is so even if the Act is unreasonable or if it was produced by fraud (*British Railways Board v Pickin* (1974)).

3 However, where an Act is in conflict with European Union legislation, then the EU law takes priority (*R v Secretary of State for Transport ex p Factortame (Case C-213/89 [1990] ECR 1-2433)*).

4 a) Since 2000, where an Act of Parliament is incompatible with the European Convention on Human Rights the court may make a declaration of incompatibility.

   b) This does not invalidate the Act; it simply draws the Government's attention to the problem and the Government can choose whether or not to amend the Act.

   c) In 2004 the House of Lords held that the Anti-Terrorism, Crime and Security Act 2001 was incompatible with human rights legislation. The Government then changed the law by passing the Prevention of Terrorism Act 2005.

▶ 3.5 Delegated legislation

Delegated legislation is law made by a body other than Parliament, but with Parliament's authority. That authority is given in a parent or enabling Act.

3.5.1 Types of delegated legislation

1 Orders in Council – made by the Queen and Privy Council. These can be made when Parliament is not sitting, under the with Civil Contingencies Act 2004. There is also power to give effect to EU law under the European Communities Act 1972.

2 Statutory instruments – made by Government Ministers. This is the most used type of delegated legislation.

3 Local authority by-laws – made by local councils in respect of matters in their area.

4 By-laws made by public corporations – made to regulate behaviour in such areas as London Underground.

5 Court rules – made by Court Rules Committees in respect of the various courts and their procedures.

3.5.2 Need for delegated legislation

1 There is a lack of parliamentary time for considering all necessary regulations.

2   It allows more detail to be included than is possible in an Act of Parliament.

3   There is expertise for matters requiring technical knowledge.

4   There is local knowledge for local by-laws.

5   It allows more time for consultation.

6   It is easier to amend than an Act of Parliament.

3.5.3 Control of delegated legislation

Parliamentary	Judicial
Enabling Act sets parameters	Can be challenged in the courts under the doctrine of *ultra vires*
Affirmative resolution requires parliamentary vote	This can be: • substantive; or • procedural
Negative resolution allows a debate to be requested	If found to be *ultra vires*, the legislation can be declared void
Delegated Powers Scrutiny Committee reports to House of Lords	
Joint Select Committee reviews statutory instruments	
Ministers can be questioned	

1   Parliament sets the parameters for the delegated legislation in the enabling Act.

2   The House of Lords' Delegated Powers Scrutiny Committee (set up in 1993) considers whether the provisions of Bills give inappropriate delegated legislative power. It reports to the House of Lords before the Committee Stage on the Bill.

3   The Joint Select Committee on Statutory Instruments reviews all statutory instruments and draws the attention of both Houses of Parliament to points that need to be considered. The main reasons for referring a statutory instrument to Parliament are:

   ● it imposes a tax;

   ● it has retrospective effect;

- it has gone beyond the powers given in the enabling Act;
- it makes unusual or unexpected use of the powers;
- it is unclear or defective in some way.

4   A few statutory instruments have to be considered and approved by Parliament under the affirmative resolution procedure. The enabling Act specifies where this is required.

5   Most statutory instruments are subject to the negative resolution procedure. This means that they will become law within 40 days unless a debate is requested by an MP.

6   If a statutory instrument (SI) is made under the power given in the Legislative and Regulatory Reform Act 2006 it can be subject to:

- a super affirmative resolution; or
- an affirmative resolution; or
- a negative resolution.

7   A super affirmative resolution means that, as well as both Houses voting on the SI, the Minister whose department issued the SI must have regard to:

- any representations by those consulted on the SI;
- any resolution of either House of Parliament;
- any recommendations by a committee of either House of Parliament which was asked to report on the draft order.

8   MPs may question the relevant Minister in Parliament about proposed delegated legislation.

9   The courts can declare void any delegated legislation which goes beyond the maker's powers, under the doctrine of *ultra vires*. (See, for example, *R v Home Secretary, ex parte Fire Brigades Union* (1995), *R v Secretary of State for Education and Employment, ex parte National Union of Teachers* (2000)).

10   Delegated legislation can also be declared *ultra vires* because the correct procedures were not followed (*Aylesbury Mushroom case* (1972)).

11   Delegated legislation can also be declared void if it is unreasonable (*Strickland v Hayes* (1896)).

3.5.4 Disadvantages of delegated legislation

1   It is undemocratic as most regulations are made by civil servants or other unelected people, except for local authority by-laws which are made by an elected council.

2 'Henry VIII' clauses can give power to delegated legislation to amend or repeal Acts of Parliament.

3 There is inadequate parliamentary control.

4 There is a lack of publicity.

5 There are too many regulations through delegated legislation.

Key Cases Checklist

Parliamentary sovereignty

***British Railways Board v Pickin* (1974)**
No court is entitled to go behind an Act once it has been passed

***R v Secretary for State for Transport, ex p Factortame* (1990)**
EU law is supreme over national law

Legislation

Delegated legislation

***R v Secretary of State for the Home Office, ex p Fire Brigades Union*(1995)**
Delegated legislation could not replace an existing statutory scheme

***Aylesbury Mushrooms Ltd* (1972)**
Where the correct procedure is not carried out, delegated legislation can be *ultra vires*

***Strickland v Hayes* (1896)**
Delegated legislation can be declared void if itis unreasonable

3.4

British Railways Board v Pickin [1974] 1 All ER 609

(HL)

Key Facts

A private Act of Parliament, the British Railways Act 1968, was enacted by Parliament. It was challenged on the basis that that the British Railways Board had fraudulently concealed certain matters from Parliament. This had led to Parliament passing the Act which had the effect of depriving *Pickin* of his land or proprietary rights. The action was struck out as frivolous.

Key Law

No court is entitled to go behind an Act once it has been passed. No challenge can be made to an Act of Parliament even if there was fraud.

3.4

R v Secretary for State for Transport, ex p Factortame (Case C-213/89) [1990] ECR 1-2433

(ECJ)

Key Facts

The UK Parliament passed the Merchant Shipping Act 1988. This Act provided that, for a fishing vessel to be registered in the UK, the majority of the ownership had to be held by UK nationals. This provision was in conflict with provisions under EU law and the Act of Parliament was held to be invalid as against EU nationals.

Key Law

Where an Act of Parliament is in conflict with EU legislation, then the EU legislation takes priority. There is supremacy of EU law over national law.

3.5.3

R v Secretary of State for the Home Office, ex p Fire Brigades Union [1995] 2 All ER 244

Key Facts

The Home Secretary set up a Criminal Injuries Compensation Scheme by prerogative order. There was a statutory scheme (under the Criminal Justice Act 1988) already in existence.

Key Law

Delegated legislation could not replace an existing statutory scheme. The Home Secretary's scheme was void.

3.5.3

Agricultural, Horticultural and Forestry Industrial Training Board v Aylesbury Mushrooms Ltd [1972] 1 All ER 280

Key Facts

Before establishing an agricultural training board, legislation obliged the Minister of Labour to consult 'any organisation appearing to him to be representative of substantial numbers of employers engaging in the activity concerned'. He failed to consult the Mushroom Growers' Association which represented about 85 per cent of all mushroom growers. As a result the order establishing a training board was invalid as against mushroom growers.

Key Law

Where the correct procedure is not carried out, delegated legislation can be *ultra vires* and invalid.

3.5.3

R v Secretary of State for Education and Employment, ex p National Union of Teachers [2000] All ER (D) 991

Key Facts

The Education Act 1996 gave the Secretary of State for Education and Employment power to set conditions for appraisal of teachers and access to higher rates of pay. The Secretary allowed only four days for consultation. In addition the scheme went beyond the powers laid down in the Act. The scheme was held to be void, on both substantive and procedural grounds.

1) Where insufficient time is allowed for consultation, the delegated legislation is procedurally *ultra vires*.

2) Where delegated legislation goes beyond the powers given in the enabling Act, it is substantively *ultra vires*.

3.5.3   *Strickland v Hayes* [1896] 1 QB 290   DC

Key Facts

A byelaw prohibiting the singing or reciting of any obscene song or ballad, and the use of obscene language generally, was held to be unreasonable as it was not limited to public places nor did it require the prohibited acts to be done to the annoyance of the public.

Key Law

Delegated legislation can be declared void if it is unreasonable.

4 Statutory interpretation

Rules and approaches

Literal rule/approach
Giving words their plain, ordinary, dictionary meaning even if this leads to injustice of absurdity

Golden rule
Used where Literal rule would lead to an absurdity

Mischief rule
Looks to see what 'gap' or 'mischief' in the law the Act was passed to deal with

Purposive approach
Judges try to discover what Parliament intended and interpret the words accordingly

Intrinsic and extrinsic aids

Intrinsic
Those in the Act including
- long and short titles
- preamble
- definition sections
- schedules

Extrinsic
Those outside the Act, including
- dictionaries
- previous law
- Hansard
- Law reform reports

Statutory interpretation

Presumptions

There are presumptions:
- against a change in the common law
- that *mens rea* is required
- that the Crown is not bound
- Parliament did not intend to oust the jurisdiction of the courts
- legislation does not apply retrospectively

Rules of language

Ejusdem generis
Where a list of words is followed by a general term, then that term is limited to the same kind of things as ion the list

Expressio unius est exclusio alterius
Where there is a list of words NOT followed by a general term, then the Act applies only to the items in the list

Noscitur a sociis
Words are looked at in context

A large percentage of cases heard by the House of Lords and the Court of Appeal (Civil Division) involve the meanings of words in a statute or delegated legislation.

▶ 4.1 Need for statutory interpretation

1   Words are an imperfect means of communication.

2   There may be ambiguity – words often have more than one meaning.

3   A broad term may have been used which is not clear (*Brock v DPP* (1993) on the meaning of 'type' in the Dangerous Dogs Act 1991).

4   There may have been a drafting error or omission.

5   New developments can lead to words not covering present-day situations (*Royal College of Nursing v DHSS* (1981)).

▶ 4.2 Approaches to statutory interpretation

There is a major debate as to whether judges should interpret legislation so as to give effect to the intention or purpose of that legislation (purposive approach), or whether judges should take the words at their literal meaning (literal approach).

Literal approach

1   The literal approach gives words their plain, ordinary, dictionary meaning.

2   The literal approach is preferred by 'conservative' judges who do not believe that a judge's role is to create law.

Purposive approach

3   The purposive approach is a broader approach. Judges try to decide what Parliament was trying to achieve.

4   The purposive approach is the one favoured by activist or creative judges, such as Lord Denning.

European approach

5   The European approach to interpretation is based on the purposive approach.

6   As a result of the European influence, our courts are becoming more likely to use the purposive approach.

Comment

7   Since any of the rules or approaches can be used, it is sometimes suggested that judges simply use the rule that will give them the result they want in the case.

8   This can possibly be seen in the decision of Lord Parker in *Smith v Hughes* (1960). Lord Parker normally supported the literal approach. However, in *Smith v Hughes* he ignored the literal wording of the Act but pointed out that the Street Offences Act 1959 was passed in order to prevent prostitutes soliciting men who were on the streets.

▶ 4.3 Rules of interpretation

The courts developed three 'rules' – the Literal Rule, the Golden Rule and the Mischief Rule – for statutory interpretation. These rules have now largely been superseded by the literal versus purposive approaches, but even so they are sometimes used.

1   Literal Rule – this uses the plain, ordinary, literal, grammatical meaning of the words (*Whiteley v Chappell* (1868), *London and North Eastern Railway Co v Berriman* (1946), *Lees v Secretary of State for Social Services* (1985)).

- Where words have a technical legal meaning, then under the Literal Rule, this will be used (*Fisher v Bell* (1960)).

- 'If the words of an Act are clear, then you must follow them, even though they lead to a manifest absurdity' (Lord Esher in *R v Judge of the City of London Court* (1892)).

2   Golden Rule – this is a modification of the Literal Rule first set out in *Grey v Pearson* (1857), where the literal interpretation would lead to an absurdity. Zander has described this rule as 'an unpredictable safety-valve to permit the courts to escape from some of the more unpalatable effects of the literal rule'.

3   There are two ways in which the Golden Rule has operated in cases:

- the narrow application, where words are capable of having more than one meaning, in which case the meaning that is least absurd should be used;

- the wider application, which is used to modify words to avoid an absurdity (*Adler v George* (1964)) or to avoid a repugnant situation (*Re Sigsworth* (1935)).

4   Mischief Rule – this was first formulated in *Heydon's case* (1584). The court looks to see what gap or 'mischief' in the law the Act was passed to cover (*Smith v Hughes* (1960), *Royal College of Nursing v DHSS* (1981), *DPP v Bull* (1994)).

4.4 The purposive approach

1   This approach is the opposite to the literal rule. It looks beyond the words of the Act.

2   It is wider than the Mischief Rule as it looks to see what Parliament intended, not just what the gap in the law was (*Jones v Tower Boot Co Ltd (1997)*, *R (Quintavalle) v Secretary of State (2003)*).

3   Judges using this approach are prepared to use a wide range of extrinsic aids (see 4.6).

4   Critics of this approach claim that only the words used in the Act can show what Parliament intended.

4.5 Intrinsic aids

1   Intrinsic aids are those other parts of the Act which may help to make the meaning of the particular section clear. These are:

- the long title and the short title;
- the preamble, if any;
- definition sections;
- schedules;
- headings before any section or groups of sections.

2   Marginal notes are not generally accepted as an intrinsic aid, as they are not part of the Act as voted on by Parliament but are added at the printing stage.

4.6 Extrinsic aids

1   These are matters outside the Act in question which may be considered by the courts. Extrinsic aids that are fully accepted are:

- dictionaries;
- historical setting;
- previous Acts of Parliament;
- earlier case law.

2   Reference to *Hansard* is now allowed (*Pepper v Hart (1993)*, *Wilson v First County Trust Ltd (No 2) (2003)*), but only where:

- the legislation is ambiguous or obscure; and

- the material relied on consists of statements made by a Minister or other promoter of the Bill; and

- the statements relied on are clear.

3   Where the court is interpreting law that was passed to give effect to an international Convention or a European Directive, then *Hansard* can be used more widely. The court may consider ministerial statements even if the statute does not appear to be ambiguous or obscure (*Three Rivers District Council and others v Bank of England (No 2)* (1996)).

4   Law reform reports by bodies such as the Law Commission may be considered, but only to discover the 'mischief' or gap in the law with which the legislation based on the report was designed to deal (*Black Clawson case* (1975)). However, in *R v G and another* (2003), the House of Lords considered the Law Commission's Report which led to the passing of the Criminal Damage Act 1971, pointing out that the meaning of 'reckless' was made plain in it.

5   International Conventions and any *travaux préparatoires* material issued in relation to the convention may be considered when considering the meaning of English legislation based on the Convention (*Fothergill v Monarch Airlines Ltd* (1980)).

❯ 4.7 Rules of language

These are rules to aid interpreting certain formats of words. If the particular format is not used, then the rule has no relevance. The rules are:

- *ejusdem generis* – where a list of words is followed by general words, then the general words are limited to the same kind of items as those in the list (*Hobbs v CG Robertson Ltd* (1970)) – there must be at least two types in the list in order for this rule to be used (*Allen v Emmerson* (1944));

- *expressio unius est exclusio alterius* – the mention of one thing excludes another; where there is a list of words which is not followed by general words, then the Act applies only to the items in the list (*Tempest v Kilner* (1846));

- *noscitur a sociis* – a word is known by the company it keeps; words must be looked at in their context (*Inland Revenue Commissioners v Frere* (1965)).

▶ 4.8 Presumptions

The courts will make certain presumptions about the law, but these are only a starting point. If the Act expressly or by implication states that the presumption will not apply, then it does not.

The main presumptions are:

- against a change to the common law;
- that *mens rea* is required;
- the Crown is not bound unless the statute expressly says so;
- Parliament did not intend to oust the jurisdiction of the courts;
- legislation does not apply retrospectively.

▶ 4.9 The European approach

1 The purposive approach to interpretation is favoured by most European legal systems. Consequently, the European Court of Justice takes this approach.

2 In *Henn and Derby v DPP* (1981), Lord Diplock contrasted this with the English courts' approach, saying that the European Court of Justice 'seeks to give effect to what it perceives to be the spirit rather than the letter of the Treaties'.

3 The Treaty of Rome requires Member States to 'take all appropriate measures ... to ensure the fulfilment of the obligations' under the Treaty. This encourages the courts in Member States to use the purposive approach.

4 Where a European Directive has been issued, 'national courts are required to interpret their national law in the light of the wording and the purpose of the directive' (*von Colson v Land Nordrhein-Westfalen* (1984)).

5 As a result, when deciding points of law that involve European law, the English courts are using the purposive approach.

6 There has also been a gradual move towards a greater use of the purposive approach in other cases before the English courts (*Pepper v Hart* (1993)).

▶ 4.10 The effect of the Human Rights Act 1998

1   Section 3 of the Human Rights Act 1998 requires courts in England and Wales, as far as is possible, to read and give effect to legislation in a way which is compatible with the rights in the European Convention on Human Rights.

2   This has been done in a number of cases. For example, in *Attorney-General's Reference No 4 of 2002* (2004) the House of Lords held that s 11 of the Terrorism Act 2000 could be read as imposing an evidential burden rather than a legal burden regarding the defendant proving he was not a member of a proscribed terrorist group.

3   In some cases the courts have given very wide interpretations in order to comply with the Convention. For example, in *Ghaidan v Godin-Mendoza* (2002) it was held that the words in the Rent Act 1977 'as his or her wife or husband' could be read as meaning 'as if they were his or her wife or husband', in order to comply with the Convention rights in respect of sexual discrimination and give protection to same-sex relationships.

▶ 4.11 The judicial role in interpretation

1   Traditionalist judges favour the passive role in interpretation, believing that they should apply the law as shown by the words, and not 'fill in the gaps' in legislation.

2   This view was expressed by Viscount Dilhorne: 'If language is clear and explicit, the court must give effect to it, for in that case the words of the state speak for the intention of the legislature' (*Kammins Ballroom Co Ltd v Zenith Investments Ltd* (1970)).

3   Activist judges favour the purposive approach to interpretation and see their role as a more creative one.

4   Lord Denning was a major supporter of the activist role: 'We sit here to find out the intention of Parliament and carry it out, and we do this better by filling in the gaps and making sense of the enactment than by opening it up to destructive analysis' (*Magor and St Mellons RDC v Newport Corporation* (1950)).

5   This statement was criticised by Lord Simonds in the same case on appeal to the House of Lords, when he said that it was 'a naked usurpation of the legislative function under the thin guise of interpretation'.

6   The decision in *Pepper v Hart* (1993) on the use of *Hansard* showed a move towards a more activist role although there are limitations on its use.

7   It is yet to be seen whether the Supreme Court will be more activist than the former House of Lords.

8   However, the courts in general appear to be using a more activist approach. For example, in *R(Ghai) v Newcastle upon Tyne City Council* (2010), where the Court of Appeal took a 'generous' rather than 'restricted' meaning of the word 'building' in the Cremation Act 1902.

Key Cases Checklist

Literal rule

***R v Judge of the City of London* (1892)**
The literal meaning of the word should always be taken even if the result is absurd

***Fisher v Bell* (1960)**
***Whitely v Chappell* (1868)**
The literal meaning of words in both these cases led to an absurd result

***London & North Easter Railway Co v Berriman* (1946)**
An example of an unjust decision through the use of the literal rule

***Magor and St Mellons RDC v Newport Corp* (1950)**
Literal rule used but judges disagreed on its use

Golden rule

***Grey v Pearson* (1857)**
Literal meaning to be used unless it leads to absurdity or repugnance

***Adler v George* (1964)**
Words modified to avoid an absurd result

***Re Sigsworth* (1935)**
Literal meaning NOT used as it would have been repugnant

Statutory interpretation

Mischief rule

***Heydon's Case* (1584)**
The courts should consider the gap the Act was passed to correct

***Smith v Hughes* (1960)**
Mischief rule used rather than literal meaning of words

***Royal College of Nursing v DHSS* (1981)**
Application of the mischief rule to prevent the 'mischief' of back-street abortions

***DPP v Bull* (1994)**
Reports can be looked at to discover the mischief

Purposive approach

***Jones v Tower Boot Co Ltd* (1997)**
Interpretation should promote the purpose of Parliament

***R (Quintavalle) v Secretary of State* (2003)**
The law should give effect to Parliament's purpose where there were later scientific developments

4.3

R v Judge of the City of London Court [1892] 1 QB 273

Key Facts

The court had to decide whether the City of London Court had jurisdiction to hear the case under the County Courts Admiralty Jurisdiction Acts. If so this would give the court power to ward up to £300 in damages. If not, then the maximum damages would be £50.

Key Law

The words of the Acts were given their literal meaning.

Key Judgment: Lopez LJ

'I have always understood that, if the words of an Act are unambiguous and clear, you must obey those words, however absurd the result may appear; and, to my mind, the reason for this is obvious. If any other rule were followed, the result would be that the court would be legislating instead of the properly constituted authority of the country, namely, the legislature.'

4.3

Fisher v Bell [1960] 1 QB 394

Key Facts

D was a shop-keeper who had displayed a flick knife marked with a price in his shop window; but had not actually sold any. He was charged under s 1(1) of the Restriction of Offensive Weapons Act 1959. The section made any person who sells or hires or offers for sale or hire a flick-knife guilty of an offence. The court had to decide whether he was guilty of offering the knife for sale. There is a technical legal meaning in contract law of 'offer'. This has the effect that displaying an article in a shop window is not an offer; it is only an invitation to treat. The Court of Appeal held that under the literal legal meaning of 'offer', the shop-keeper had not made an offer to sell and so was not guilty of the offence.

Key Law

A literal interpretation was used.

Key Comment

In this case, the outcome was clearly not what Parliament intended as they amended the law by the Registration of Offensive Weapons Act 1961 to cover the display of knives in shop windows.

4.3

Whiteley v Chappell (1868) 4 LR QB 147

Key Facts

D was charged under a section which made it an offence to impersonate 'any person entitled to vote'. D had pretended to be a person whose name was on the voters' list, but who had died. The court held that D was not guilty since a dead person is not, in the literal meaning of the words, 'entitled to vote'.

Key Law

A literal interpretation was used, even though it meant D was acquitted.

4.3

London & North Eastern Railway Co v Berriman [1946] 1 All ER 255   HL

Key Facts

Mr Berriman was a railway worker who was hit and killed by a train while doing maintenance work, oiling points on a railway line. A regulation made under the Fatal Accidents Act stated that a look-out should be provided for men working on or near the railway line 'for the purposes of relaying or repairing' it. Mr Berriman was not relaying or repairing the line; he was maintaining it. His widow claimed compensation for his death because the railway company had not provided a look-out man while Mr Berriman had to work on the line. It was held that the relevant regulation did not cover maintenance work, so Mrs Berriman's claim failed.

Key Law

A literal interpretation was used, even though the regulations were intended to improve safety for those working on railway lines.

Magor and St Mellons RDC v Newport Corporation [1950] 2 All ER 1226

 HL

Key Facts

The Newport Extension Act 1934 extended the county borough of Newport to include the areas of Magor and St Mellons. The Act provided that these two Rural District Councils should receive reasonable compensation. Immediately after the Act took effect, the two Rural District Councils were amalgamated to form a new District Council. The court had to decide whether this new Council had a right to compensation. It was held that it had no right.

Key Law

A literal interpretation of the law was used.

Key Comment

This case is important for the conflict between Lord Denning in his dissenting judgment in the Court of Appeal and the judgment of the House of Lords, as shown in these quotes:

Key Judgment: Lord Denning

'We sit here to find out the intention of Parliament and carry it out, and we do this better by filling in the gaps and making sense of the enactment than by opening it up to destructive analysis.'

Key Judgment: Lord Scarman

'If Parliament says one thing but means another, it is not, under the historic principles of the common law, for the courts to correct it. The general principle must surely be acceptable in our society. We are to be governed not by Parliament's intentions but by Parliament's enactments.'

4.3   ### *Grey v Pearson* (1857) 6 HL Cas 61

 HL

Key Facts

The facts and decision are not important in the context of statutory interpretation. The significant point of the case is the definition of the golden rule in Lord Wensleydale's judgment.

Key Judgment: Lord Wensleydale

'[T]he grammatical and ordinary sense of the words is to be adhered to, unless that would lead to some absurdity or some repugnance or inconsistency with the rest of the instrument, in which case the grammatical and ordinary sense of the words may be modified, so as to avoid that absurdity and inconsistency, but no further.'

4.3   *Adler v George* [1964] 1 All ER 628   DC

Key Facts

D was prosecuted under the Official Secrets Act 1920 for an offence of obstructing HM forces 'in the vicinity of' a prohibited place. D had obstructed HM forces but was inside the prohibited place. The Divisional Court read the Act as being 'in or in the vicinity of' and held that D was guilty.

Key Law

The golden rule was used to modify the words of the Official Secrets Act 1920, in order to avoid the absurdity of being able to convict someone who was near (in the vicinity of) a prohibited place but not being able to convict someone who carried out the obstruction in the place.

4.3   *Re Sigsworth* [1935] Ch 89   HC

Key Facts

A son had murdered his mother. The mother had not made a will, so normally her estate would have been inherited by her next of kin, according to the rules set out in the Administration of Justice Act 1925. This meant that the murderer-son would have inherited as her 'issue'. There was no ambiguity in the words of the Act, but the court held that the literal meaning of the word should not apply. The son could not inherit.

Key Law

The golden rule can be used to prevent a repugnant situation. Here it was the repugnancy of the son inheriting.

Key Comment

The court was, in effect, writing into the Act that the 'issue' would not be entitled to inherit where they had killed the deceased.

This result of the case would also be achieved by applying the purposive approach (see 3.5).

4.3

Heydon's Case (1584) Co Rep 7a

The facts and decision are not important in the context of statutory interpretation. The significant point of the case is the definition of the mischief rule.

Key Law

In interpretation of a statute, there are four points the court should consider. In the original language of the case these are:

> '1st What was the Common Law before the making of the Act.
>
> 2nd What was the mischief and defect for which the Common Law did not provide.
>
> 3rd What remedy the Parliament hath resolved and appointed to cure the disease of the commonwealth.
>
> And, 4th The true reason of the remedy; and then the office of all Judges is always to make such construction as shall suppress the mischief, and advance the remedy.'

4.3

Smith v Hughes [1960] 2 All ER 859

Key Facts

Six women had been convicted under s 1(1) of the Street Offences Act 1959 which stated that 'It shall be an offence for a common prostitute to loiter or solicit in a street or public place for the purpose of prostitution'. In each case they argued on appeal that they were not 'in a street or public place' as required by the Act for them to be guilty. One woman had been on a balcony and the others had been at the windows of ground floor rooms, with the window either half open or closed. In each case the women were attracting the attention of men by calling to them or tapping on the window. The court decided that they were guilty.

Key Law

The court should look at the mischief which the Act was designed to prevent.

Key Judgment: Lord Parker CJ

'For my part I approach the matter by considering what is the mischief aimed at by this Act. Everybody knows that this was an Act to clean up the streets, to enable people to walk along the streets without being molested or solicited by common prostitutes. Viewed in this way it can matter little whether the prostitute is soliciting while in the street or is standing in the doorway or on a balcony, or at a window, or whether the window is shut or open or half open.'

Key Link

Eastbourne Council v Stirling [2000] EWHC Admin 410.

4.3   *Royal College of Nursing v DHSS* **[1981] 1 All ER 545**   HL

Key Facts

Under s 1(1) of the Abortion Act 1967, abortion is legal 'when a pregnancy is terminated by a registered medical practitioner' in specific circumstances. When the Act was passed in 1967 the procedure to carry out an abortion was by surgery so that only a doctor (a registered medical practitioner) could do it. In 1973 a new medical technique allowed pregnancy to be terminated by inducing premature labour with drugs.

The first part of the procedure for this was carried out by a doctor, but the second part could be performed by nurses without a doctor present. The Department of Health and Social Security issued a circular giving advice that it was legal for nurses to carry out the second part of the procedure. The Royal College of Nursing sought a declaration that the circular was wrong in law. It was held to be lawful.

Key Law

The application of the mischief rule was preferred to the literal rule.

Key Judgment: Lord Diplock

'The Abortion Act 1967 which it falls to this House to construe is described in its long title as "An Act to amend and clarify the law relating to termination of pregnancy by registered medical practitioners". Whatever may be the technical imperfections of its draftsmanship, however, its purpose in my view becomes clear if one starts by considering what was the state of the law relating to abortion before the passing of the Act, what was the mischief that required amendment, and in what respect was the existing law unclear.'

Key Comment

The decision that the procedure was lawful under the Abortion Act 1967 was made by a three to two majority. The dissenting judges were very opposed to the decision. Lord Edmund Davies stated that to read the words 'terminated by a registered medical practitioner' as meaning 'terminated by treatment for the termination of pregnancy in accordance with recognised medical practice' was redrafting the Act 'with a vengeance'.

4.3   ***DPP v Bull* [1994] 4 All ER 411**   DC

Key Facts

Bull was a male prostitute charged with an offence against s 1(1) of the Street Offences Act 1959. The case was dismissed by the magistrate on the ground that the words 'common prostitute' only applied to female prostitutes. The prosecution appealed by way of case stated. The Divisional Court considered the Wolfenden Report, Cmnd 247, 1957, which had led to the passing of the Act. That report clearly identified the mischief as being one created by women. The court held that the words were only meant to apply to women. They did not cover male prostitutes.

Key Law

A report may be considered in order to discover the mischief an Act was intended to remedy.

4.4

Jones v Tower Boot Co Ltd [1997] 3 All ER 406   CA

Key Facts

The complainant suffered verbal and physical abuse from two fellow employees because of his racial background. He claimed his employers were liable for this conduct under s 32(1) of the Race Relations Act 1976 which provides that:

> *'Anything done by a person in the course of his employment shall be treated for the purposes of the Act . . . as done by his employer as well as by him, whether or not it was done with the employer's knowledge or approval.'*

The employers argued that they were not liable as racial abuse was not within the course of employment. This was supported by the principles of vicarious liability in the law of tort. The court pointed out that the purpose of the Act was to eradicate racial discrimination and held that the employers were liable.

Key Law

The interpretation should be such as to promote the purpose of Parliament.

Key Comment

The decision in this case can be contrasted with that in *Fisher v Bell* (see 4.3) where a special legal meaning of the words in the law of contract was taken, even though this was clearly not what Parliament had intended in the criminal law. Here the special legal meaning of the words was rejected in favour of the purpose of Parliament.

4.4

R (Quintavalle) v Secretary of State [2003] UKHL 13   HL

Key Facts

The issue was whether organisms created by cell nuclear replacement (CNR) came within the definition of 'embryo' in the Human Embryology and Fertilisation Act 1990. Section 1(1)(a) states that 'embryo means a live human embryo where fertilisation is complete'. CNR was not possible in 1990 and the problem is that fertilisation is not used in CNR. It was held that CNR did come within the definition of 'embryo'.

Key Law

The courts should give effect to Parliament's purpose.

Key Judgment: Lord Bingham

'[T]he court's task, within permissible bounds of interpretation is to give effect to Parliament's purpose . . . Parliament could not have intended to distinguish between embryos produced by, or without, fertilisation since it was unaware of the latter possibility.'

Extrinsic aids

Black Clawson Case (1975)
Reports leading to the passing of an Act maybe considered in order to identify the mischief the new law was intended to remedy

R v R and G (2003)
Law Commission report considered in overruling a earlier case

Fothergill v Monarch Airlines (1980)
Travaux préparatoires can be considered where the law implements an International Convention

Pepper v Hart (1993)
Hansard may be considered if the legislation is ambiguous or obscure or leads to an absurdity

Wilson v First County Trust (2003)
Consulting Hansard is not contrary to the Bill of Rights

Statutory interpretation

Rules of language

Hobbs v CG Robertson Ltd (1970)
Where there is a list followed by a general term, the general term is limited to items of the same nature as the list

Allen v Emmerson (1944)
There must be at least two specific types in the list for the rule to apply

Tempest v Kilner (1846)
A list not followed by a general term is limited to the items in the list

Inland Revenue v Frere (1965)
Words must be considered in their context

4.6

Black-Clawson International Ltd v Papierwerke Waldhof-Aschaffenburg AG [1975] 1 All ER 810

HL

Key Facts

There was a dispute over the enforcement of a foreign judgment which involved the interpretation of s 8(1) of the Foreign Judgments (Reciprocal Enforcement) Act 1933. The court had to decide whether it could look at a report which had led to the passing of the Act. It held that it could do so in order to discover the mischief which the Act had been passed to remedy.

Key Law

Where there is an ambiguity in a statute, the court may have regard to a report which resulted in the passing of the Act in order to ascertain the mischief the Act was intended to remedy.

Key Link

DPP v Bull [1994] 4 All ER 411.

4.6

R v R and G [2003] UKHL 50

HL

Key Facts

Two young boys set fire to some newspapers in a shop yard. After they left the fire spread to the shop itself and to other shops. They were charged with arson under the Criminal Damage Act 1971. The court had to decide the meaning of 'reckless' in the Act. Prior to the passing of the Act there had been a report by the Law Commission. However, in *Metropolitan Police Commissioner v Caldwell* (1981), the House of Lords had refused to look at the report but instead gave an objective meaning to recklessness (i.e. that a defendant would be guilty if an ordinary adult would have realised the risk). The court consulted the report and overruled *Caldwell* holding that the report showed that subjective recklessness was required.

Key Law

Reports leading to the passing of legislation can be considered by the courts.

Key Judgment: Lord Bingham

'[S]ection 1 as enacted followed, subject to an immaterial addition, the draft proposed by the Law Commission. It cannot be supposed that by "reckless" Parliament meant anything different from the Law Commission. The Law Commission's meaning was made plain both in its Report (Law Com No 29, 1970) and in Working Paper No 23 which preceded it. These materials (not, it would seem, placed before the House in *R v Caldwell*) reveal a very plain intention to replace the old expression "maliciously" by the more familiar expression "reckless" but to give the latter expression the meaning which *R v Cunningham* [1957] 2 QB 396 had given to the former . . . No relevant change in the *mens rea* necessary for the proof of the offence was intended, and in holding otherwise the majority misconstrued section 1 of the Act.'

4.6

Fothergill v Monarch Airlines Ltd [1980] 2 All ER 696

Key Facts

The case involved interpretation of the Carriage by Air Act 1961 and the Warsaw Convention 1929 which was contained in a schedule to the Act. The court held it could look at *travaux préparatoires* (explanatory notes published with the Convention) in order to understand its true effect.

Key Law

The original Convention should be considered along with any preparatory materials or explanatory notes published with an International Convention as it was possible that, in translating and adapting the Convention to our legislative process, the true meaning of the original might have been lost.

4.6

Pepper (Inspector of Taxes) v Hart [1993] 1 All ER 42   (HL)

Key Facts

Teachers were charged reduced fees for their children at an independent school. This concession was a taxable benefit. The question was exactly how the calculation of the amount to be taxed should be done. Under the Finance Act this had to be done on the 'cash equivalent' of the benefit. Section 63 of the Finance Act 1976 defined 'cash equivalent' as 'an amount equal to the cost of the benefit, and further defined the 'cost of the benefit' as 'the amount of any expense incurred in or in connection with its provision'. This was ambiguous as it could mean either:

a) the marginal (or additional) cost to the employer of providing it to the employee (this on the facts was nil) (the decision); or

b) the average cost of providing it to both the employee and the public (this would involve the teachers having to pay a considerable amount of tax).

Key Law

Hansard could be consulted on the intention of Parliament when passing an Act of Parliament.

Key Judgment: Lord Browne-Wilkinson

'The exclusionary rule should be relaxed so as to permit reference to parliamentary materials where; (a) legislation is ambiguous or obscure, or leads to an absurdity; (b) the material relied on consists of one or more statements by a minister or other promoter of the Bill together if necessary with such other parliamentary material as is necessary to understand such statements and their effect; (c) the statements relied on are clear. Further than this I would not at present go.'

4.6

Wilson v First County Trust Ltd (No 2) [2003] UKHL 40   (HL)

Key Facts

The Speaker of the House of Commons and the Clerk of the Parliament were joined in the case to make representations against the use of Hansard for the purpose of deciding compatibility of an Act with the European Convention on Human Rights. The court held that *Hansard* could be consulted, though in the actual case *Hansard* did not provide any assistance with interpretation.

Key Law

Consulting *Hansard* did not amount to a 'questioning' of what is said in Parliament and so was not contrary to s 1 of Art 9 of the Bill of Rights 1688.

Key Judgment: Lord Nicholls

'The courts would be failing in the due discharge of the new role assigned to them by Parliament if they were to exclude from consideration relevant background information whose only source was a ministerial statement in Parliament or an explanatory note prepared by his department while the Bill was proceeding through Parliament.

By having such material the court would not be questioning proceedings in Parliament or intruding improperly into the legislative process or ascribing to Parliament the views expressed by a minister. The court would merely be placing itself in a better position to understand the legislation.'

Key Comment

It is noticeable that the judgment extends beyond *Hansard* as it clearly states, *obiter*, that the court also has a duty to consider explanatory notes.

4.7

Hobbs v CG Robertson Ltd [1970] 1 WLR 980

 CA

Key Facts

Hobbs, a workman, had injured his eye when brickwork which he was removing splintered. He claimed compensation under the Construction (General Provision) Regulation 1961. These regulations made it a duty for employers to provide goggles for workmen when 'breaking, cutting, dressing or carving of stone, concrete, slag or similar material.suffered an eye injury from a piece of brick as he was removing. His claim failed.

Key Law

Where there are specific words followed by a general term, the general term is limited to the same kind of items as the specific words. Brick was a soft material and not *ejusdem generis* with the list in the regulations.

4.7   *Allen v Emmerson* [1944] All ER 344   DC

Key Facts

The court had to interpret the phrase 'theatres and other places of amusement' and decide if it applied to a funfair. As there was only one specific word 'theatres', it was decided that a funfair did come under the general term 'other places of amusement' even though it was not of the same kind as theatres.

Key Law

There must be at least two specific categories for the *ejusdem generis* rule to operate.

4.7   *Tempest v Kilner* (1846) 3 CB 249

Key Facts

The court had to consider whether the Statute of Frauds 1677, which required a contract for the sale of 'goods, wares and merchandise' of more than £10 to be evidenced in writing, applied to a contract for the sale of stocks and shares. The list 'goods, wares and merchandise' was not followed by any general words, so the court held that only contracts for those three types of things were affected by the statute; because stocks and shares were not mentioned they were not caught by the statute.

Key Law

Where there is a list of words which is not followed by general words, then the legislation applies only to the items in the list.

4.7

Inland Revenue Commissioners v Frere [1965] AC 402

HL

Key Facts

The section of the relevant Income Tax Act set out rules for 'interest, annuities or other annual interest'. The first use of the word 'interest' on its own could have meant any interest paid, whether daily, monthly or annually. Because of the words 'other annual interest' in the section, the court decided that 'interest' only meant annual interest.

Key Law

Words must be looked at in context and interpreted accordingly. This may involve looking at other words in the same section or at other sections in the Act.

5 European Union law

```
THE INSTITUTIONS

Council – government representatives
Commission – 27 independent commissioners
Parliament – 785 directly elected MEPs
```

```
EUROPEAN UNION
```

```
SOURCES OF LAW

Treaties – directly applicable
Regulations – directly applicable
Directives – vertical direct effect
```

```
EFFECT ON SOVEREIGNTY

EU law takes priority over national law
Van Gend en Loos (1963)
Factortame (1990)
```

The European Union (originally the European Economic Community) was founded in 1957 with six members. The United Kingdom joined in 1973 and by 1995 Union membership increased to 15. Another ten countries joined on 1 May 2004 and two more countries in 2007, making a total of 27 Member States.

The founding treaty was the Treaty of Rome 1957. This has now been replaced with two treaties: the Treaty on European Union (TEU) and the Treaty on the Functioning of the European Union (TFEU).

▶ 5.1 The institutions

5.1.1 The Council of the European Union

1   The Council is attended by a government representative of each Member State who must be 'at ministerial level, authorised to commit the government of that Member State' (Article 16 TEU).

2   The Presidency is held by each Member State in rotation for a period of six months.

3   The Council is the principal decision-making body of the Union.

4   Sensitive areas such as taxation and social security must be decided by a unanimous vote.

5   For most other matters decisions are made by a qualified majority on a weighted voting basis. Each state has a set number of votes based on its population size.

5.1.2 The Commission

1   There are 27 Commissioners who are appointed for a five-year term, one from each Member State.

2   Commissioners must act in the best interests of the Union. They must 'refrain from any activity incompatible with their duties' (Article 245 TFEU).

3   The Commission is the motivating force behind Union policy. It proposes policies and presents drafts of legislation to the Council for consideration by the Council.

4   The Commission is also the 'guardian of the treaties' and ensures that treaty provisions and other measures are implemented by Member States.

5   The Commission may refer an infringement by a Member State to the European Court of Justice (Article 258 TFEU).

6   It also has investigative powers over alleged infringements (Article 245 TFEU).

7   It is responsible for the administration of the Union and has executive powers to implement the Union's budget.

5.1.3 The Parliament

1   Members of the Parliament are elected by the citizens of the Member States. Elections take place once every five years. There are 78 MEPs from the UK.

2   The Parliament has no direct law-making authority. Its role is to discuss proposals and put questions to the Council and the Commission.

3   However, it has some important control functions. It has power to dismiss the Commission by passing a vote of censure (Article 234 TFEU). In 1999 the entire Commission resigned to forestall such a censure vote.

4   The Parliament has some power over the budget, especially on non-necessary expenditure.

5   Under Article 228 TFEU, the Parliament may appoint an Ombudsman to receive complaints of maladminstration by the Union institutions. The first Ombudsman was appointed in 1995.

5.1.4 Other representative bodies

1   The Economic and Social Committee advises the Commission and the Council on economic matters.

2   It consists of 'representatives of organisations of employers, of the employed, and of other parties' representative of civil society, notably in socio-economic, civic, professional and cultural areas' (Article 300 TFEU).

3   The Committee of the Regions advises the Commission and the Council on regional matters.

5.1.5 The Court of Justice of the European Union

1   The function of the court is 'to ensure that in the interpretation and application of the Treaty the law is observed' (Article 19 TEU).

2   There are 27 judges (one from each Member State) who are appointed from those eligible for appointment to the highest judicial posts in their own country (Article 252 TFEU).

3   The court is assisted by eight Advocates-General whose task is to research all the legal points involved and 'to present publicly, with complete impartiality and independence, reasoned conclusions on cases submitted to the Court of Justice with a view to assisting the latter in the performance of its duties' (Article 253 TFEU).

4   The court has wide jurisdiction over Union law. It hears cases brought by the institutions, Member States or individuals alleging a breach of Union law. A main area here is the role of the Commission in bringing cases against Member States.

5   It also hears cases referred by courts in any Member State for a preliminary ruling on a point of Union law (Article 267 TFEU).

6   Such referrals are mandatory where no further appeal is possible in the Member State's court system and discretionary from any other court.

7   The Court of Justice of the European Union operates in a different way to English courts. The main differences are:

- cases are presented on paper with only limited oral argument;

- an Advocate-General is used to present an independent view of the law;

- judgments are always given in a written form as the decision of the whole court; it is never revealed if there were any dissenting judges;

- the court is not bound by its own previous decisions;

- the court uses the purposive approach to interpretation.

▌ 5.2 Sources of law

Source	Effect	Cases
Treaties	Directly applicable Have both vertical and horizontal direct effect	*Van Duyn* (1974) *Macarthys v Smith* (1980)
Regulations Art 288 TFEU	Directly applicable Have both vertical and horizontal direct effect	*Re Tachographs* (1979) *Leonesio* (1972)
Directives Art 288 TFEU	Have vertical direct effect Do *NOT* have horizontal direct effect Can sue State under *Francovich* principle	*Marshall* (1986) *Duke v GEC* (1988) *Francovich* (1991)
Recommendations and opinions Art 288 TFEU	'Soft' law Must be taken into considertation when interpreting law	*Grimaldi* (1989)

Effect of the different sources of law

5.2.1 Treaties

1   Treaties are the primary source of European Union law.

2   All Treaties are 'without further enactment to be given legal effect or used in the United Kingdom' (s 2(1) European Communities Act 1972).

3   Treaties are therefore directly applicable and, where a Treaty creates individual rights, then those rights can be relied on by an individual (*Van Duyn v Home Office* (1974), *Macarthys Ltd v Smith* (1980)).

5.2.2 Regulations

1   Regulations are issued under Article 288 TFEU.

2   This makes the effect of Regulations 'binding in every respect and directly applicable in each Member State'.

3   Member States must enforce Regulations; they have no choice over whether to bring them into effect (*Commission v UK: Re Tachographs* (1979)).

4   Regulations have vertical and horizontal direct effect. This means that citizens may rely on them both against the State and against other private individuals or bodies (*Leonesio v Ministero dell'Agricoltura* (1972)).

5.2.3 Directives

1   Directives are issued under Article 288 TFEU.

2   Directives 'bind any Member State to which they are addressed as to the result to be achieved, while leaving to domestic agencies a competence as to form and means'.

3   They are issued with a time limit for implementation in the Member States. If a Directive is not implemented it will have vertical direct effect when the time limit for implementation expires. So where the Directive creates individual rights, those rights may be relied on against the State or an 'arm of the State' (*Marshall v Southampton and South West Hampshire Area Health Authority* (1986)).

4   The concept of an 'arm of the State' is a body that has been made responsible for providing a public service under the control of the State (*Foster v British Gas plc* (1990)).

5   However, Directives that have not been implemented do not have horizontal direct effect. They cannot be relied on against private individuals or bodies (*Duke v GEC Reliance Ltd* (1988), *Dori v Recreb Srl* (1994)).

6   Where a Directive has not been implemented, an individual who suffers loss as a result of the non-implementation may sue the State for their breach of Community law (*Francovich v Italian Republic* (1991)).

7   In *Dori v Recreb Srl* (1994) the European Court of Justice held that compensation would be payable where:

- the purpose of the Directive was to grant rights to individuals;
- those rights could be identified from the Directive;
- there was a causal link between the breach of the State's obligations and the damage suffered.

8   In *R v HM Treasury, ex parte British Telecommunications plc* (1996) the court said that compensation would be payable only where the breach was sufficiently serious.

5.2.4 Recommendations and Opinions

1   These are also issued under Article 288 TFEU. Neither creates enforceable rights.

2   However, national courts are bound to take them into consideration when interpreting national law adopted to give effect to a Recommendation (*Grimaldi v Fondes des Maladies Professionelles* (1989)).

3   This effect is known as 'soft law', as opposed to the 'hard law' effect of legislation with binding force.

▶ 5.3 Effect on sovereignty of Parliament

5.3.1 Conflict between EU law and national law

1   In *Van Gend en Loos* (1963), where there was a conflict between the Treaty of Rome and an earlier Dutch law, the European Court of Justice said that 'the Member States have limited their sovereign rights, albeit within limited fields, and have created a body of law which binds both their nationals and themselves'.

2   In *Costa v ENEL* (1964) there was a conflict between a number of Treaty provisions and a later Italian law, which under Italian law would take priority. The European Court of Justice held that 'The reception, within the laws of each Member State, of provisions having a Community source . . . has as a corollary the impossibility, for the Member State, to give preference to a unilateral and subsequent measure . . .'.

3   In *Internationale Handelsgesellschaft mbH* (1970) the court held that an EU regulation that conflicted with the German constitution took precedence over the German law.

4   In *Simmenthal SpA (No 2)* (1979) the court stated that national courts are under a duty to give full effect to the provisions of EU law and, if necessary, should refuse to apply national laws that conflict with EU law.

5.3.2 Sovereignty of Parliament

1   The fact that EU takes precedence over national law means that while the UK is a member of the Union, Parliament is no longer the supreme law-maker.

2   This was stressed when the validity of the Merchant Shipping Act 1988 was successfully challenged as it conflicted with the Treaty of Rome (*R v Secretary of State for Transport, ex parte Factortame* (1990)).

3   Domestic courts are under a duty to apply EU law in preference to national law.

Key Cases Checklist

Effect of EU sources of law

Van Duyn v Home Office (1974)
Treaties can confer rights on which individuals can rely

Macarthys v Smith (1979)
An individual can enforce a right in EU law

Commission v UK: Re Tachograph (1979)
EU regulations are binding in their entirety on Member States

Marshall v Southampton and South-West Hampshire Area Health Authority (1986)
Directives have vertical direct effect and can be relied on by individuals against the State

Duke v GEC Reliance Ltd (1988)
Directives do not have horizontal direct effect and cannot be relied on against a private organisation or individual

Grimaldi v Fond des Maladies Profes-sionelles (1989)
Recommendations do not have binding effect but must be taken into account by national courts

European Union Law

Supremacy of EU law

Van Gend en Loos v Nederlandse Administratie (1963)
EU law takes precedence over national law

R v Secretary of State for Transport, ex p Factortame (1990)
EU law is supreme over national law even when the national law has been passed subsequent to the relevant EU law

5.2

Van Duyn v Home Office [1975] 3 All ER 190 ECJ

Key Facts

The UK refused to allow a member of the Church of Scientology to enter the country. This contravened the freedom of movement of workers under what was then Art 39 of the Treaty of Rome, but the UK relied on the right to derogate on the grounds of public policy as contained in Directive 64/221. It was held that the Treaty conferred individual rights which could be relied on, but, in the circumstance of this case, the UK could derogate from those rights.

Key Law

Individuals can rely in English law on rights given by the Treaties setting out European Union Law.

5.2

Macarthys v Smith [1979] WLR 1189 ECJ

Key Facts

A woman discovered that she was being paid less than her less-qualified male predecessor in the job. She was the only one doing that work in the company and therefore could not rely on English law as there was no male comparator. She claimed discrimination under what was then Art 141 of the Treaty of Rome (as worded prior to the reworking of the Treaty under the Treaty of Amsterdam). It was held that the she could rely directly on the Treaty.

Key Law

Primary legislation (treaties) of the European Union which conferred rights on individuals was of direct effect and could be relied on, even when national law was contrary to EU law.

5.2

Commission v UK: Re Tachographs [1979] ECR 419

 ECJ

Key Law

Council Regulation EEC/1463/70 made it compulsory for tachographs (mechanical recording equipment) to be fitted to certain types of vehicle. The UK brought the regulation into effect through a Statutory Instrument which provided for a voluntary system of fitting tachographs. It was held that the fitting was compulsory.

EU Regulations are directly binding in their entirety. They cannot be applied by Member States in an incomplete or selective manner.

5.2

Marshall v Southampton and South West Hampshire Area Health Authority [1986] 2 All ER 584

ECJ

Key Facts

The applicant, a woman, had been forced to retire before the age of 65, while men were allowed to work until that age. A reference was made to the European Court of Justice (now the Court of Justice of the European Union) on the point of whether this amounted to discrimination under the Equal Access Directive 76/207. The court held that the rights conferred by the Directive could be relied on as against the State.

Key Law

Directives have vertical direct effect.

5.2

Duke v GEC Reliance Ltd [1988] 1 All ER 626   HL

Key Facts

The facts were the same as in *Marshall* (above). However, the employer was a private body and not the state. It was held that the Directive did not give rights against private bodies.

Key Law

....

Directives do NOT have horizontal direct effect.

5.2   ***Grimaldi v Fond des Maladies Professionelles***
[1989] ECR 4407

Key Facts

....

A Belgian tribunal made a reference to the European Court of Justice as to the standing of a Commission recommendation. It was held that national courts, when deciding a case, must take relevant recommendations into account.

Key Law

....

Recommendations do not have binding effect but must be taken into account.

5.3.1   ***Van Gend en Loos v Nederlandse***
***Administratie* [1963] ECR 1**   ECJ

Key Facts

....

It was held that a re-classification of import duties by the Dutch Government contravened the then Art 12 of the Treaty of Rome.

Key Law

....

EU law takes precedence over national law.

5.3.2   ***R v Secretary for State for Transport,***
***ex p Factortame* [1990] ECR 1-2433, [1991]**
1 All ER 70   ECJ

Key Facts

....

The Merchant Shipping Act 1988 was passed by Parliament to protect British fishing. It required that the majority ownership of a company had to be in the hands of UK nationals for a ship to be registered to fish in British waters. It was held that this contravened the 'non-discrimination on nationality' rule in the then Art 12 of the Treaty of Rome.

Key Law

EU law is supreme over national law.

Key Judgment: Judge Rapporteur, CN Kakouris

'[A]ny provision of a national legal system and any legislation, administrative, or judicial practice which might impair the effectiveness of Community law . . . are incompatible with those requirements which are the very essence of EC law.'

Need for law reform

- Law made piecemeal
- Many obsolete statutes
- Low priority for Parliament
- Judges limited in powers to reform

LAW REFORM

Law Commission

- Established by Law Commission Act 1965
- Full-time
- Five commissioners
- Researches/consults
- Report + draft Bill
- Many reforms
- Failure to codify
- 70% of reports enacted

Other law reform bodies

- Law Reform Committee
- Criminal Law Revision Committee
- Royal Commissions, eg Phillip Commission
- Various *ad hoc* committees and
- reviews, eg Woolf Review

▶ 6.1 The need for law reform

1 English law has developed in a piecemeal fashion; there is no code of law, unlike in many European countries.

2 Judges can only reform law on individual points that come before the courts as cases arise (eg *R v R* (1991), making marital rape an offence).

3 Parliament has many other functions, and reform of 'lawyers' law' in particular often takes a low priority (eg the failure to implement the Draft Code of Criminal Law).

4 There are many statutes that have become obsolete, but which have never been repealed.

5 Before 1965 there were only part-time law reform bodies, such as the Law Reform Committee and the Criminal Law Revision Committee.

6 It was felt that there was a need for a full-time law reform body, so the Law Commission was created.

▶ 6.2 Law Commission

6.2.1 Composition and working

1 This was established by the Law Commissions Act 1965.

2 It is a full-time body with a chairman, who is a High Court Judge seconded to the Law Commission for a term of three years, and four other Law Commissioners.

3 Its role is:

- to systematically develop and reform the law;
- to simplify and modernise the law;
- to codify the law;
- to eliminate anomalies;
- to repeal obsolete and unnecessary enactments.

4 The Lord Chancellor may refer topics to the Law Commission, but most topics are selected by the Commission itself, which then seeks governmental approval to draft a report on the topic.

5 The area of law is researched, then a consultation paper is published setting out the current law, the problems with it and possible options for reform.

6   After consultation, the Commission will draw up positive proposals for reform. These will be presented in a report which will also set out the research that led to the conclusions.

7   A draft Bill may be attached to the report showing precisely how the law should be reformed.

6.2.2 Implementation of reports

1   Overall about 70% of the Law Commission's reports have eventually led to legislation.

2   However, the rate has not been consistent. In the first ten years 85% of reports were enacted by Parliament. In the next ten years only 50% became law. In 1990 not one proposal was made law.

3   In the early 1990s a Special Standing Committee of the House of Lords considered Law Commission draft Bills and this led to an increase in the number of reports which were implemented.

4   The lack of parliamentary commitment to law reform has been frequently commented on by successive chairmen of the Law Commission in their annual reports.

5   A major area that has been ignored by Parliament is the reform of the criminal law. In 1985 a Draft Criminal Code was published by the Law Commission. No part of this was ever implemented by Parliament.

6   In 2008 the Law Commission stated that it would be concentrating on smaller areas of the code, as there was more chance that the Government would be prepared to make such reforms of the law.

7   In the last ten years the Government has implemented many Law Commission reports.

6.2.3 Achievements of the Law Commission

1   Many Acts of Parliament have been enacted as the result of Law Commission reports.

2   Examples include:

- Occupiers' Liability Act 1984;
- Law Reform (Year and a Day Rule) Act 1996;
- Contract (Rights of Third Parties) Act 1999;
- Land Registration Act 2002;

- Fraud Act 2006;
- Corporate Manslaughter and Corporate Homicide Act 2007.

3   The Law Commission has also 'tidied up' the statute book with the repeal of over 2,500 obsolete statutes.

▶ 6.3 Other law reform bodies

1   The part-time Law Reform Committee still contributes to law reform of civil law (eg Latent Damage Act 1986) and is consulted by the Law Commission on certain areas, eg trust law.

2   The part-time Criminal Law Revision Committee sat from 1957 to 1987 and one of its main achievements was the reform of the law of theft and related offences in the Theft Act 1968.

3   Temporary commissions or committees are used to review one specific area of law or the legal system. These are often chaired by a judge, with the commission being referred to by the name of that judge. Some of their proposals may become law. Examples include:

- the Royal Commission on Police Procedure (Phillips Commission 1981), which led to the Police and Criminal Evidence Act 1984;

- the Royal Commission on Criminal Justice (Runciman Commission 1993), some of whose recommendations were implemented in the Criminal Appeal Act 1995 and the Criminal Procedure and Investigations Act 1996;

- the Woolf Review of the civil justice system, which led to the Civil Procedure Rules 1999 and wide-ranging reform of the system.

4   Judges and business people are increasingly being asked to review areas of the legal system and the law, eg David Clementi's review on the provision of legal services (2004), Lord Carter's review on legal funding in 2006 and Lord Jackson's review of litigation costs in 2009.

7 The civil justice system

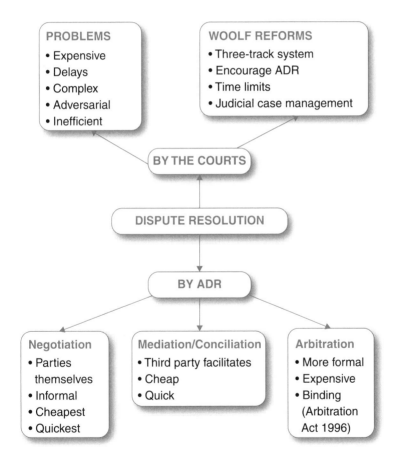

PROBLEMS
- Expensive
- Delays
- Complex
- Adversarial
- Inefficient

WOOLF REFORMS
- Three-track system
- Encourage ADR
- Time limits
- Judicial case management

BY THE COURTS

DISPUTE RESOLUTION

BY ADR

Negotiation
- Parties themselves
- Informal
- Cheapest
- Quickest

Mediation/Conciliation
- Third party facilitates
- Cheap
- Quick

Arbitration
- More formal
- Expensive
- Binding (Arbitration Act 1996)

Civil justice has always been seen as too expensive and too complex, with long delays. In 1999, the Woolf reforms of the civil justice system tried to address these problems.

▶ 7.1 The court structure

7.1.1 The three tracks

All cases that are defended are allocated to one of three tracks.

1   Small claims track – this is for most cases under £5,000. Note that the normal limit for housing disrepair cases and personal injury cases is £1,000, while illegal eviction and harassment cases are excluded from the small claims track. Note there are proposals to increase this limit to £10,000.

2   Fast track cases – these are claims for between £5,000 and £25,000, although cases of this amount involving a complex point of law can be allocated to the multi-track.

3   Multi-track cases – these are claims over £25,000, or complex cases for less than this amount.

7.1.2 The civil courts

1   There are two civil courts that hear cases at first instance. These are the County Court and the High Court.

2   The County Court hears all small claims cases and all fast track cases. County Courts, which are designated as Civil Trial Centres, can also deal with multi-track cases above £25,000. However, unless the parties agree, cases above £50,000 in value are not usually tried in the County Court.

3   The High Court has three divisions.

   ● Queen's Bench Division – for contract and tort claims; there are also special courts in the Commercial List, Technology and Construction List, and in the Admiralty Court.

   ● Chancery Division – for disputes involving matters such as mortgages, trusts, copyright and patents; winding up of companies is dealt with by the Companies Court within this Division.

   ● Family Division – for family-related disputes, wardship cases and cases relating to children under the Children Act 1989. Note the Crime and Courts Act 2013 has provision for a separate Family Court to be created.

▶ 7.2 Procedure in outline

1   The **Civil Procedure Rules 1999** set out the rules for each stage of a case.

2   The overriding objective of the Rules is to enable the court to deal with cases justly, by:

- ensuring that the parties in any case are on an equal footing;
- dealing with cases in a way which is proportionate to the amount involved and the importance of the case.

3   Parties are encouraged to disclose the facts of their case prior to starting any court case. For some types of claim (eg personal injury) a pre-action protocol must be followed.

4   All claims for less than £25,000 must be started in the County Court. Claims for more than this amount can be started in either the High Court or the County Court, except personal injury claims for less than £50,000, which must be started in the County Court.

5   Most types of claim are started by issuing a Part 7 claim form. Particulars of a claim must be included on the claim form, or attached to it, or served separately within 14 days of the claim form being served.

6   There must also be a statement of truth as to the facts in the particulars of the claim.

7   The claim form and the particulars of the claim must be served on the defendant. This may be done by the court or the claimant and can be served personally, by post, by fax, by e-mail or other electronic means.

8   The defendant has 14 days in which to respond. A defendant may:

- pay the claim;
- admit or partly admit it;
- file an acknowledgement of service (but then must file a defence within another 14 days);
- file a defence.

9   A defence that just denies the claim is not sufficient; it should be more specific.

10 At any point before or after the commencement of proceedings, the defendant or the claimant may make a Part 36 offer (to settle) and payment.

7.2.1 Allocation of cases

1   When a defence is filed at court, an allocation questionnaire is sent to all parties. This helps the judge decide which track the case should be allocated to.

2   An allocation fee has to be paid at this stage, but not for claims under £1,500.

3   If a party is dissatisfied with the allocation decision, an application can be made to the court for the claim to be re-allocated.

7.2.2 Small claims procedure

1   Cases are heard by a District Judge, who will normally use an interventionist approach.

2   Cases are dealt with in a relatively informal way.

3   The use of lawyers is discouraged because the winning party cannot recover the costs of using a lawyer from the losing side.

4   There may be a paper adjudication if the judge thinks it is appropriate and the parties agree.

7.2.3 Fast track cases

1   The concept of the fast track was described by Lord Woolf as 'intended to provide improved access to justice . . . by providing a strictly limited procedure designed to take cases to trial in a short but reasonable timescale at a fixed cost'.

2   There are standard directions by the court for trial preparation.

3   There should be a maximum delay of 30 weeks between directions and trial. Unfortunately this target has not yet been achieved. Waiting times are usually about 50 weeks.

4   Normally only one expert witness is allowed and, if the parties cannot agree on an expert, the court has power to appoint one. The expert's evidence will be given in writing.

5   There are fixed costs for the advocate at the trial.

7.2.4 Multi-track cases

1   There is no standard procedure for pre-trial directions; the judge has flexibility to use a number of different approaches, including case management conferences and pre-trial reviews.

2   The aim is to identify the issues as early as possible and, where appropriate, try specific issues prior to the main trial. This is aimed at encouraging a settlement.

3   The number of expert witnesses is controlled by the court as the court's permission is needed for any party to use an expert to give evidence (oral or written).

4   All time limits are strictly enforced (*Vinos v Marks and Spencer plc* (2001)). An approximate date for the trial (a 'trial window') is given to the parties and the court is very unlikely to agree to any adjournment.

▶ 7.3 Encouraging ADR

1   The Civil Procedure Rules state that 'Active case management' includes encouraging parties to ADR to resolve disputes (CPR 1.4(2)(e)).

2   If there is a clause in a contract agreeing to arbitration or to try ADR in the event of a dispute, then any court proceedings may be stayed (*Avery v Scott* (1856), *Cable & Wireless plc v IBM* (2002)).

3   Where parties unreasonably refuse to try ADR, the court can decline to award costs (*Dunnett v Rail Track plc* (2002), *Halsey v Milton Keynes General NHS Trust* (2004), *Burchell v Bullard* (2005)).

▶ 7.4 Appeals

7.4.1 Appeal routes

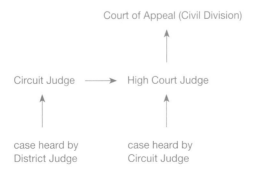

Appeals in small claims and fast track cases

1   Since 2000 appeals may be made in small claims cases under Rule 52 CPR; the route is for an appeal from a decision by a District Judge to go

to a Circuit Judge. Appeals for small claims were introduced in order to comply with the European Convention on Human Rights.

2   Appeals for fast track cases depend on which level of judge heard the case. An appeal from a District Judge goes to a Circuit Judge; an appeal from a Circuit Judge goes to a High Court Judge.

3   A second appeal to the Court of Appeal (Civil Division) may only be made where the Court of Appeal considers that:

a) the appeal would raise an important point of principle or practice;

or

b) there is some other compelling reason for the Court of Appeal to hear it (s 55(1) Access to Justice Act 1999).

This has the effect that second appeals for small claims or fast track cases will become a rarity (*Tanfern Ltd v Cameron-Macdonald* (2000)).

Supreme Court

Court of Appeal (Civil Division)

All appeals from High Court
and
County Court multi-track cases

Appeals in multi-track cases

4   Appeals from the final decision in a multi-track case heard in the County Court go to the Court of Appeal.

5   All appeals from decisions of the High Court go to the Court of Appeal. The exception to this is where an appeal is made direct to the Supreme Court under the leapfrog procedure (Administration of Justice Act 1969).

6   In a multi-track case where there has been an appeal to the Court of Appeal, then a further appeal to the Supreme Court is possible.

7.4.2 The approach to appeals

1   Permission to appeal is usually required; this can be from either the trial court or the relevant appeal court.

2 Permission will only be granted where the court considers that:

- an appeal would have a real prospect of success; or

- there is some other compelling reason why the appeal should be heard.

3 The prospect of success must be realistic rather than fanciful (*Swain v Hillman* (1999)).

4 Permission to appeal is not required where the liberty of the individual is in issue, eg an appeal against a committal order.

5 Rule 52.11 states that an appeal will only be allowed (ie successful) where the decision of the lower court was wrong or where it was unjust because of a serious procedural or other irregularity.

▶ 7.5 Comment on the post-Woolf civil system

1 It is generally felt that the reforms are a qualified success.

2 The adversarial approach has been replaced by more co-operation between parties, and the use of ADR has increased.

3 The real issues of cases are being defined more quickly and this is leading to more cases settling and earlier settlements (rather than 'court door' settlements on the day of the trial).

4 The main problems are that:

- the system is heavily front loaded, both in work to be done and in cost;

- the new procedures, such as pre-action protocols, allocation questionnaires and case management conferences, are more complex.

5 There is a less adversarial culture and a greater willingness to 'put cards on the table', with insurance companies more prepared to settle.

6 The main disadvantages include:

- in PI cases front loading of work means that costs have gone up;

- delay is not improved as solicitors do more work before opening negotiations.

▶ 7.6 Alternative dispute resolution

7.6.1 Negotiation

1   This is an informal approach between the parties themselves or their lawyers.

2   It is completely private and is the quickest and cheapest method of resolving a dispute.

7.6.2 Mediation/conciliation

1   Mediation is a process in which a neutral person (the mediator) helps the parties reach a compromise solution to their dispute. The mediator will discuss the position of each party with them and what outcomes they want from the dispute, but will not usually offer an opinion. The emphasis is on the parties themselves working out a solution.

2   Conciliation goes beyond mediation in that the mediator (or conciliator) has power to suggest grounds for compromise and the possible basis for a settlement.

3   There are a number of mediation/conciliation services, eg the Centre for Dispute Resolution.

4   ADR allows the parties to have control over the resolution process as they can withdraw at any time and a solution cannot be imposed on them – they must agree to it.

5   The process is preferred to court proceedings as it is:

- cheaper;
- quicker;
- more informal;
- conducive to business relations remaining more amicable between the parties.

6   The main disadvantage is that neither mediation nor conciliation will necessarily lead to an agreement.

7.6.3 Arbitration

1   This is the voluntary submission by the parties of their dispute to the judgment of an arbitrator (or panel of arbitrators) who is neutral.

2   The agreement to arbitrate is usually in writing, and written arbitration agreements are governed by the Arbitration Act 1996.

3   The agreement to go to arbitration can be made before a dispute arises (usually by a *Scott v Avery* clause in a contract) or after the dispute has arisen.

4   The agreement will either name an arbitrator or provide a method of choosing one. If the parties cannot agree on an arbitrator the court can be asked to appoint one (Arbitration Act 1996).

5   The procedure for the arbitration hearing agreed by the parties can range from a 'paper' arbitration to a very formal court-like procedure.

6   The decision by the arbitrator is called an award. It is binding on the parties and can be enforced through the courts if necessary.

7   An award by an arbitrator can only be challenged in the courts on the grounds of serious irregularity in the proceedings or on a point of law (ss 68, 69 Arbitration Act 1996).

8   The main advantages of arbitration are:

- expertise – where the arbitrator has specialist knowledge;
- flexibility – ability to choose time, place and type of procedure;
- privacy – the facts of the dispute are not made public;
- speed – although commercial and international arbitrations are subject to delays;
- cost – although the use of specialist arbitrators can be expensive.

9   The main disadvantage is that legal points are not suitable for decision by a non-lawyer.

Key Cases Checklist

Civil Procedure

Rules
Rule 1.1(1)
The overriding objective is to enable the court to deal with cases justly

Rule 1.4
The court must further the overriding objective by actively managing cases

Timetables

***Vinos v Marks & Spencer plc* (2001)**
Time limits set out in the CPR are to be strictly observed

Civil Courts and Procedure

Encouraging ADR

***Scott v Avery* (1856)**
Ifthere is an agreement to arbitrate, court proceedings will be stayed

***Cable & Wireless plc v IBM* (2002)**
A specific clause agreeing to go to ADR is enforceable

***Dunnett v Railtrackplc*(2002)**
Failure to use ADR can lead to cost penalties

***Halsey v Milton Keynes General NHS Trust* (2004)**
Costs normally follow the event but unreasonable refusal to try ADR can lead to departure from this rule

***Burchell v Bullard* (2005)**
The parties cannot ignore a proper request to mediate simply because it was made before the claim was issued

Overriding objective

Civil Procedure Rules

....

Rule 1.1(1)

'These rules are a new procedural code with the overriding objective of enabling the court to deal with cases justly.'

Civil Procedure Rules

Rule 1.2

'Dealing with a case justly includes, so far as practicable:

(a) ensuring that the parties are on an equal footing;

(b) saving expense;

(c) dealing with the case in ways which are proportionate to:

  (i)   the amount of money involved;

  (ii) the importance of the case;

  (iii) the complexity of the issues; and

  (iv) the financial position of each party;

(d) ensuring that it is dealt with expeditiously and fairly; and

(e) allotting to it an appropriate share of the court's resources, while taking into account the need to allot resources to other cases.'

Case management

Civil Procedure Rules

Rule 1.4

'(1) The court must further the overriding objective by actively managing cases.

(2) Active case management includes:

  (a) encouraging the parties to co-operate with each other in the conduct of the proceedings;

  (b) identifying the issues at an early stage;

  (c) deciding promptly which issues need full investigation and trial and accordingly disposing summarily of the others;

  (d) deciding the order in which issues are to be decided;

  (e) encouraging the parties to use an alternative dispute resolution procedure if the court considers that appropriate and facilitating the use of such procedure;

  (f) helping the parties settle the whole or part of the case;

(g) fixing timetables or otherwise controlling the progress of the case;

(h) considering whether the likely benefit of taking a particular step justify the cost of taking it;

(i) dealing with the case without the parties needing to attend court;

(j) making use of technology; and

(k) giving directions to ensure that the trial of a case proceeds quickly and efficiently.'

Timetables

7.2.4

Vinos v Marks & Spencer plc [2001] 3 All ER 784

Key Facts

The claimant (V) had suffered injuries at work. After lengthy attempts to negotiate a settlement failed, V's solicitors issued court proceedings one week before the expiry of the limitation period. They did not serve these proceedings on D until nine days after the end of the four-month period set down in the Civil Procedure Rules. They applied for an extension of time. The court refused the extension.

Key Law

Time limits set out in the CPR are to be strictly observed.

Encouraging ADR

7.3

Scott v Avery (1856) 5 HL Cas 811

Key Facts

Insurance policies in respect of a ship included clauses that stated (1) that any 'difference' should be referred to arbitration and (2) that any party who refused to refer the matter to arbitration could not bring or continue a claim on the policy in the courts. One party brought a court action, but the court held that such clauses were lawful and stayed the case.

Key Law

Where there is an agreement to go to arbitration, any court proceedings will be stayed.

7.3

Cable & Wireless plc v IBM [2002] EWHC 2059 Comm

HC

Key Facts

The parties had an agreement under which IBM was to supply information technology. In the event of a dispute, the agreement contained the following clause:

'If the matter is not resolved by negotiation, the parties shall attempt in good faith to resolve the dispute or claim through an Alternative Dispute Resolution (ADR) procedure as recommended to the parties by the Centre for Dispute Resolution. However, an ADR procedure which is being followed shall not prevent any party from issuing proceedings.'

A dispute arose and the claimants issued proceedings and refused to go through any ADR procedure. The judge held the clause was enforceable and stayed the proceedings for ADR to be attempted.

Key Law

A clause in an agreement to go to ADR in the event of a dispute can be binding on the parties. The clause must be more than an agreement to negotiate.

7.3

Dunnett v Railtrack plc [2002] EWCA Civ 303, [2002] 2 All ER 850

CA

Key Facts

Following judgment in favour of the claimant, the judge granted Ds leave to appeal, but urged them to try ADR rather than use the appeal process. Ds refused to try ADR. Their appeal was successful, but the Court of Appeal refused to grant them their costs because of their refusal to consider using ADR.

Key Law

Failure to use ADR can lead to cost penalties.

Key Judgment: Brooke LJ

'Schooled mediators are now able to achieve results satisfactory to both parties in many cases which are quite beyond the power of lawyers and courts to achieve.'

7.3

Halsey v Milton Keynes General NHS Trust [2004] EWCA Civ 576

CA

Key Facts

This involved a claim for criminal negligence which it was alleged caused the death of the claimant's husband. C's solicitors repeatedly invited Ds to submit the matter to mediation. Ds repeatedly refused, as they correctly predicted that they were not liable. The claimant argued that even though she had lost the appeal, she should not be ordered to pay all Ds' costs because of their refusal to mediate. The Court of Appeal granted Ds' costs but laid down general principles on when cost penalties should be incurred.

Key Law

1) Costs normally follow the event. To depart from this rule it must be shown that the successful party acted unreasonably in refusing to agree to the use of ADR.

2) Factors to be taken into account in deciding whether the rejection of ADR is unreasonable include:

   ● the nature of the dispute;

   ● the merits of the case;

   ● the extent to which other settlement methods have been attempted;

   ● whether the costs of the mediation would be disproportionately high;

   ● whether delay in setting up mediation would be prejudicial;

   ● whether the mediation had a reasonable prospect of success.

7.3   *Burchell v Bullard* [2005] EWCA Civ 358   (CA)

Key Facts

This involved a building dispute over an extension to Ds house. Prior to issuing proceedings, C proposed ADR but D refused to consider this. The court was asked to apply a costs penalty. The court found that the factors in Halsey (see above) were present but that they would not apply a costs penalty as the refusal to use ADR had occurred prior to the decisions in *Dunnett v Railtrack plc* (2002) and *Halsey v Milton Keynes General NHS Trust* (2004).

Key Law

The parties cannot ignore a proper request to mediate simply because it was made before the claim was issued.

Key Comment

The court refused to apply CPR 7.6 as it only allows for an extension if:

a) the court has been unable to serve the claim form; or

b) the claimant has taken all reasonable steps to serve the claim form but has been unable to do so; and

c) in either case the claimant has acted promptly in making the application.

None of these applied in the *Vinos* case.

The court also refused to use CPR 3.10 which gives the court a general power to remedy an error of procedure. It was not appropriate as it would be in contradiction to the specific rule in CPR 7.6(3).

Godwin v Swindon Borough Council [2001] EWCA Civ 1478, [2001] 4 All ER 641   (CA)

Key Facts

A claim form arrived at the defendant's address for service within the time limit. However, because of a 'deeming' provision in CPR 6.7(1) it was deemed to have arrived three days late. The court held that service was out of time.

Key Law

The deemed day of service was not rebuttable by evidence showing that service had actually been effected in time.

Key Link

Anderton v Clwyd County Council [2002] EWCA Civ 933, [2002] 3 All ER 813.

8 Tribunals and inquiries

Administrative

- Created by statute
- Enforcement of social and welfare rights, eg
  a) social security
  b) employment
  c) immigration etc.
- Usually panel of three
- More informal and cheaper than court

Domestic tribunals

- Internal disciplinary
- Some created by statute, eg Solicitors Disciplinary Tribunal
- Some have right of appeal to Privy Council

TRIBUNALS

Control of tribunals

1 Administrative Justice and Tribunals Council
- created by the Tribunals, Courts and Enforcement Act 2007
- keep system under review
- makes proposals for change
2 The Courts
- judicial review
- three prerogative orders
  a) mandatory order
  b) prohibitory order
  c) quashing irder

Inquiries

- Set up to investigate a specific issue
- May be set up under a statutory power
- Fact-finding exercise
- Work of statutory inquiries is reviewed by the Administrative Justice and Tribunals Council

▶ 8.1 Administrative tribunals

A system of tribunals operates alongside the court system. Each type of tribunal specialises in a certain type of case. Cases concerning these particular matters must go to the appropriate tribunal and not to a court.

8.1.1 History of tribunals

1   During the second half of the twentieth century, different tribunals were set up to deal with people's rights in a variety of administrative areas such as benefits for disability, rent, education, employment and immigration.

2   There were over 70 different tribunals operating in about 2,000 panels around the country.

3   There was no uniformity. Each tribunal developed its own rules.

4   There was no consistent appeal route. For some tribunals there was no appeal route. Other tribunals had a special appeal tribunal, such as the Employment Appeal Tribunal.

5   This unsatisfactory system was criticised in the Leggatt Report (2001).

8.1.2 The unified tribunal system

1   Following the Leggatt Report, the Tribunals, Courts and Enforcement Act 2007 set up a new tribunal system.

2   There is a First Tier Tribunal to hear cases at first instance.

3   The First Tier Tribunal sits in seven chambers, each chamber specialising in certain types of case, such as social entitlement, health, education and social care cases, asylum and immigration cases or taxation cases.

4   The appeal route from the First Tier Tribunal is to the Upper Tribunal.

5   From the Upper Tribunal there is a further possible appeal route to the Court of Appeal and from here to the Supreme Court.

6   Note that employment tribunals are not yet included in the new unified system. They remain separate and have their own appeal route.

8.1.3 Composition and procedure

1   The proceedings are heard by a tribunal judge. Selection of tribunal judges is made by the Judicial Appointments Commission.

2   For some topics two lay members will sit with the judge to make the decision. These lay members will have expertise in the particular field of the tribunal.

2   Most have been set up by the particular institution, although some have been established by statute, such as the Solicitors Disciplinary Tribunal under the Solicitors Act 1974.

3   Where the tribunal was established by statute, there will usually be an appeal route from its decisions. For example, an appeal from the decision by the General Medical Council to strike off a doctor can be made to the Judicial Committee of the Privy Council.

4   All are subject to the laws of natural justice and their decisions may be judicially reviewed.

▶ 8.4 Inquiries

1   Inquiries are set up as and when necessary to investigate a specific issue.

2   Some inquiries may be set up under a statutory power, eg under s 49 of the Police Act 1996 the Home Secretary can do so for any matter connected to policing in an area. This power was used to set up the Macpherson Inquiry in the Stephen Lawrence case (1997–98).

3   Even if there is no statutory power, Parliament may resolve to set up an inquiry into any matter of public importance. Often a judge will be appointed to head such an inquiry, eg the Scott Inquiry into the sale of arms to Iraq (1996) and the inquiry by Dame Janet Smith into the Shipman murders (2004).

4   Inquiries will sit in public unless this is against the public interest. They have the power to call witnesses and order the production of relevant documents or other evidence.

5   They are a fact-finding exercise and will issue a report on the matter; they cannot make any decision on any of the issues. Their findings may, however, be used as the basis for reforming the law.

6   Inquiries are subject to judicial review. They cannot go beyond their remit, as shown in *R v Chairman of Stephen Lawrence Inquiry, ex parte A* (1998), where the inquiry could not put certain questions to witnesses as its task was to examine the conduct of the police investigation into the murder of Stephen Lawrence and not to conduct a trial of the people suspected of the murder.

Key Cases Checklist

8.2.2   *Ridge v Baldwin* [1963] 2 All ER 66   HL

Key Facts

A police Chief Constable was suspended from his post when he was charged with conspiracy to obstruct the course of justice and corruption. He was acquitted on all charges. He then applied to be re-instated as Chief Constable. The Watch Committee dismissed him on the ground of neglect of duty, without giving him an opportunity to be heard. He successfully applied for a declaration that his dismissal was illegal, *ultra vires* and void.

Key Law

The rule of natural justice that both sides must be heard before a decision was made had to be observed. In this case the Chief Constable had not been given any opportunity to put his side of the matter before the Watch made their decision to dismiss him.

8.2.2   *Director General of Fair Trading v The Proprietary Association of Great Britain* [2001] 1 WLR 700 (see Key Cases in Chapter 13 on the Judiciary).   CA

9 Police powers

	POLICE POWERS	
Power	**Statutory provision**	**Comment**
Stop and search	• ss 1–7 PACE • also under other Acts, eg Misuse of Drugs Act 1971	• only in place to which the public have access • must have reasonable grounds for suspecting stolen or prohibited goods
Search of premises	• by search warrants (s 8 PACE) • to arrest someone (s 17 PACE) • after arrest (ss 18 and 32 PACE) • breach of the peace	• magistrates issue warrant • warrant must be shown before search
Arrest	• with a warrant • a constable can arrest for any offence but must have reasonable grounds for believing that it is necessary (s 24 PACE)	• magistrates issue warrant • warrant must be shown as soon as practicable after arrest
Detention	• ss 34–36 PACE • 24 hours normal limit • for indictable offences this can be extended to 96 hours with magistrates' permission	Detainee has right to: • have someone informed • have legal advice • see a copy of the Codes of Practice
Interviews	• s 53 PACE • ss 34–39 Criminal Justice and Public Order Act 1994 places limits on right to silence	• must be tape-recorded • those under 17 or vulnerable must have an appropriate adult present

▶ 9.1 Stop and search

9.1.1 Powers to stop and search

1   A police constable may stop and search people and vehicles in a place to which the public has access (s 1 PACE 1984).

2   A place to which the public has access includes a place where they have paid for entry; it also includes a garden or yard of a private property where the constable has reasonable grounds for believing that the person does not reside there and has not got the permission of the resident to be there.

3   In order to stop a vehicle the constable must be in uniform (s 2(9)(b) PACE).

4   In order to search a person or vehicle the constable must have reasonable grounds for suspecting that he will find stolen or prohibited articles (s 1(3) PACE).

5   Police officers also have specific powers to stop and search under other legislation such as the Misuse of Drugs Act 1971 and the anti-terrorism legislation.

9.1.2 Safeguards on the power to stop and search

1   If a constable is not in uniform then he must produce documentary evidence that he is a police officer.

2   In all cases, before commencing the search the constable must state his name and station to the suspect, specify the object of the proposed search and the grounds for proposing the search.

3   If this is not done then the search is unlawful (*Osman v DPP* (1999)).

4   If the search is in public, the constable can only request the removal of an outer coat, jacket and gloves (s 2(9)(a) PACE).

5   Code of Practice A gives the police guidance on the use of the stop and search powers. In particular it points out that reasonable suspicion can never be supported on the basis of personal factors alone. Factors such as age, colour, hairstyle, manner of dress or a known previous conviction cannot be used as the sole basis on which to search.

❱ 9.2 Searching premises

9.2.1 Search warrants

1   A search warrant can be issued by a magistrate allowing police to search premises.

2   Under s 8 PACE, such a warrant will only be issued where there are reasonable grounds for believing that:

- an indictable offence has been committed; and

- there is material on the premises which is likely to be of substantial value to the investigation of the offence; and

- the material is likely to be relevant evidence; and

- it is not practicable to communicate with any person entitled to grant entry to the premises or the material; or

- entry to the premises will not be granted unless a warrant is granted; or

- the purpose of the search may be frustrated or seriously prejudiced unless a constable arriving at the premises can gain immediate entry.

3   Search warrants can also be granted under other Acts. These include powers to search for stolen goods, drugs or firearms.

4   A warrant can be a 'specific premises' warrant to search a named address or it can be an 'all premises' warrant which allows all premises occupied or controlled by the defendant to be searched.

5   A search warrant can provide for access on more than one occasion.

9.2.2 Other powers to enter premises

1   Police may enter without a search warrant to arrest a person (on a warrant), or for an indictable offence, or to recapture an escaped prisoner (s 17 PACE).

2   If a person is arrested, the police can enter and search premises that were occupied or controlled by him (s 18 PACE).

3   If a person is arrested, the police can enter and search premises in which he was at the time of arrest or immediately before the arrest (s 32 PACE).

4   There is a common law right to enter premises in order to prevent or deal with a breach of the peace. This right exists even though the breach of the peace is in private property (*McLeod v Commissioner of Police of the Metropolis* (1994)).

5   The police may enter and search any premises where the occupier consents to this.

9.2.3 Safeguards on police powers to search premises

1   Where a warrant has been issued the police are required to enter and search at a reasonable hour, unless the purpose of the search might be frustrated (s 16(4) PACE and Code of Practice B para 5).

2   The police must identify themselves to the occupier of any premises searched: they must show the search warrant to him and give him a copy (s 16(5) PACE). However, this need not be done on entry, but must be done before any search commences (*R v Longman* (1988)).

3   Where the entry is under s 17 or s 18, the police must give anyone present in the premises the reason for the entry. If they do not do so the entry is unlawful (*O'Loughlin v Chief Constable of Essex* (1998)).

4   The police can only exercise powers to enter and search under s 32 immediately after arrest (*R v Badham* (1987)).

▶ 9.3 Powers of arrest

9.3.1 Powers of arrest

1   The Serious Organised Crime and Police Act 2005 amended s 24 of PACE so that the category of arrestable offence is abandoned. Instead, a constable can make an arrest for any offence.

- Section 24(1) of PACE states that a constable may arrest without a warrant:
  - a)   anyone who is about to commit an offence;
  - b)   anyone who is in the act of committing an offence;
  - c)   anyone whom he has reasonable grounds for suspecting to be about to commit an offence;
  - d)   anyone whom he has reasonable grounds for suspecting to be committing an offence.

- Section 24(2) of PACE states that if a constable has reasonable grounds for suspecting that an offence has been committed, he may arrest without a warrant anyone whom he has reasonable grounds to suspect of being guilty of it.

- Section 24(3) of PACE states that if an offence has been committed, a constable may arrest without a warrant:

  a) anyone who is guilty of the offence; or

  b) anyone whom he has reasonable grounds for suspecting to be guilty of it.

2   However, a constable can only arrest if he has reasonable grounds for believing that it is necessary to make the arrest for one of the following reasons:

- to enable the person's name or address to be ascertained;
- to prevent the person from:
    - causing physical injury to himself or any other person;
    - suffering physical injury;
    - causing loss of or damage to property;
    - committing an offence against public decency;
    - causing an unlawful obstruction of the highway;
- to protect a child or other vulnerable person;
- to allow the prompt and effective investigation of the offence or of the conduct of the person;
- to prevent any prosecution for the offence from being hindered by the disappearance of the person in question.

3   Code of Practice G gives guidelines on making arrests. It points out that a lawful arrest requires two elements:

  a) a person's involvement or suspected involvement or attempted involvement; and

  b) reasonable grounds for believing that the person's arrest is necessary.

4   If the arrest is not necessary, then it is unlawful (*Hayes v Chief Constable of Merseyside* (2011), *Richardson v The Chief Constable of West Midlands Police* (2011)).

5   Code G also points out that arresting officers are required to inform the person arrested that they have been arrested, even if this fact is obvious, and of the relevant circumstances in respect to both elements (*Taylor v Chief Constable of Thames Valley Police* (2004)).

9.3.2 Arrests with a warrant

1   An application for a warrant for arrest may be made under s 1 Magistrates' Court Act 1980.

2   The application must be supported by written information and also by sworn oral evidence showing that the person has committed or is suspected of committing an offence punishable by imprisonment.

3   A warrant must name the person to be arrested.

9.3.3 Other powers of arrest

1   There are some additional statutory powers to make an arrest, eg where a person granted police bail has failed to attend the police station on the set date (s 46A PACE).

2   There is still a common law power to arrest for breach of the peace.

9.3.4 Procedure on arrest

1   It must be made clear to the person that they are being arrested and what the arrest is for.

2   Where necessary reasonable force may used to effect the arrest (s 117 PACE).

3   If the arrest is made by a warrant, then that warrant must be shown on demand as soon as is reasonably practicable.

4   The police may search the arrested person for anything which might be used to make an escape or for evidence relating to the offence.

5   If the search takes place in public, the police can only require the suspect to remove outer coat, jacket and gloves.

6   If the arrest is not made at a police station, the suspect must be taken to a police station as soon as practicable (s 30(1) PACE).

7   However, there may be a delay if it is necessary to carry out certain investigations immediately and the presence of the suspect is necessary in order to carry out those investigations (s 30(10) PACE).

8   If there is a delay in taking a suspect to a police station the reasons for the delay must be recorded on arrival at the police station (s 30(11) PACE).

❱ 9.4 Detention at the police station

9.4.1 Time limits and the custody officer's role

1 The normal maximum time for detention is 24 hours but this can be extended to 36 hours for indictable offences if it is authorised by an officer of the rank of superintendent or above.

2 For indictable offences applications can be made to the magistrates to extend the period up to a maximum of 96 hours.

3 Under the Terrorism Act 2006 a suspect can be detained for up to 14 days with the approval of a magistrate.

4 At the beginning of the period of detention the custody officer must inform the suspect of their rights to:

- have someone informed of the arrest (s 56 PACE);
- legal advice in private (and that advice is available free of charge) (s 58 PACE);
- consult the Codes of Practice;
- speak on the telephone for a reasonable time to one person (Code C). The suspect must be given a written notice setting out these rights.

5 In the case of an indictable offence, where it is believed that it will hinder investigations the right to have someone informed and or hinder the recovery of property the right to legal advice can be delayed for up to 36 hours.

6 Where the suspect is under 17 years old, a parent or guardian should be notified of the detention (s 34(2) Children and Young Persons Act 1933).

7 The custody officer is responsible for reviewing the detention and deciding whether the person should be detained. This must be done at the outset of the detention, then after six hours, then every nine hours (s 40 PACE).

8 A record of all events (such as visits to the cell by police officers, or interviews) must be made by the custody officer.

9.4.2 The right to legal advice

1 Research in the early 1990s showed that only a small percentage of people detained requested legal advice. In order to try to make legal advice more available Code of Practice C now sets out that:

- there must be a poster in each police station advertising the right to have legal advice;

- police officers must not dissuade a person in detention from obtaining advice;
- the custody officer must point out the right to legal advice and if the person declines to speak to a solicitor the custody officer must record the reason for the refusal.

2   Although the right to legal advice can be delayed for a maximum of 36 hours in the case of an indictable offence, the courts have held that it is only in rare cases that this right can be delayed (*R v Samuel* (1988), *R v Alladice* (1988)).

9.4.3 Interviews

1   At the start of an interview a suspect must be cautioned: 'You do not have to say anything. But it may harm your defence if you do not mention when questioned something which you later rely on in court. Anything you do say may be given in evidence'.

2   This caution emphasises that the right to silence was eroded by the Criminal Justice and Public Order Act 1994 which allows adverse inferences to be made at trial where the accused has failed in the police interview to mention facts (s 34) or to account for objects, substances or marks (s 36), or for his presence at a particular place (s 37).

3   All interviews must be tape-recorded (s 60 PACE).

4   Suspects are entitled to have a lawyer present during the interview, except where the right to legal advice has been delayed under s 58 PACE in the case of an indictable offence (Code of Practice C).

5   Suspects under 17 or those who are mentally disordered or handicapped must have an appropriate adult present during the interview, even if they appear to understand the questions (*R v Aspinall* (1999)).

6   There should be a short break at least every two hours, breaks for meal times, and the suspect must be allowed an eight-hour period of rest.

7   Once a suspect has been charged they should not be further interviewed (*Charles v Crown Prosecution Service* (2009)).

8   Code of Practice E sets out rules and guidelines for the conduct of interviews.

9   If a confession is obtained by oppression or in circumstances likely to render it unreliable, this evidence can be excluded by the trial judge (s 76 PACE).

10   Evidence can also be excluded under s 78 PACE where the police have disregarded the rules under PACE (*R v Halliwell* (2012)).

9.4.4 Searches, samples and fingerprinting

1   When detained at a police station, a non-intimate search may be made if the custody officer believes this is necessary (s 54 PACE). The search must be carried out by a person of the same sex as the suspect.

2   If a strip search involving the removal of more than outer clothing is considered necessary, then the search must:

● take place where the suspect cannot be seen by any person who does not need to be present;

● be conducted with proper regard to the sensitivity of the person and to minimise embarrassment (Code of Practice C, Annex A).

3   An intimate search consists of the physical examination of a person's body orifices, other than the mouth.

4   An intimate search must be authorised by a superintendent or above in rank who believes that there is hidden:

● an article which could cause harm; or

● a Class A drug.

5   The actual search can only be carried out by a doctor or nurse, although, where it is for an article which may cause harm and a superintendent or above in rank considers it is not practicable to wait for a doctor or nurse, then a police officer may carry out the search.

6   Where the offence being investigated is a recordable offence, the police may take fingerprints (s 60 PACE) and non-intimate samples, including hair (except pubic hair) and saliva (s 63 PACE).

7   The consent of the person should be obtained before fingerprints or non-intimate samples are taken. If consent is refused fingerprints and non-intimate samples can be taken without consent where the person is detained or charged with a recordable offence. Reasonable force can be used if necessary (s 117 PACE).

8   Intimate samples (blood, semen or any other tissue fluid, urine, pubic hair, a dental impression or a swab taken from a body orifice other than the mouth) can only be taken by a doctor or nurse (s 62 PACE). Consent is needed.

9   At the moment any fingerprints or samples taken do not have to be destroyed even if the person is not found guilty or not even charged with any offence (s 64 PACE as amended by the Criminal Justice and Police Act 2001).

10 In *R (S and Marper) v UK* (2008), the European Court of Justice ruled that the indefinite retention of samples of the innocent was a breach of human rights.

11 Samples can now only be retained for three years under the Protection of Freedoms Act 2012.

▶ 9.5 Complaints against the police

1   Any person who believes that the police have exceeded their powers may make a complaint to the police authorities.

2   The type of complaint determines how it is dealt with. Minor complaints may be informally resolved if the complainant agrees.

3   Any complaint which is not resolved must be referred to the Independent Police Complaints Commission (IPCC) which was set up by the Police Reform Act 2002.

4   When a case is referred to the IPCC, they decide how it should be investigated. The different methods of investigation are:

- independent investigation carried out by the IPCC;

- managed investigation carried out by the Professional Standards Department (PSD) of a police force under the direction and control of the IPCC;

- supervised investigation by a PSD under their own direction and control but the IPCC sets the terms of reference and the PSD must report to the IPCC;

- local investigation carried out entirely by a PSD.

9.5.1 Court actions against the police

1   Where there is an allegation that a police officer has committed a crime, eg assault, criminal proceedings may be taken against that police officer. These proceedings may be commenced by the Crown Prosecution Service or as a private prosecution by the victim.

2   Where there is a breach of civil rights, the individual affected may take civil proceedings and claim damages (compensation). For example, where the police have entered premises without a search warrant a claim for trespass to land may be made, or where there has been an unlawful arrest or unreasonable force a claim for trespass to the person may be made.

Key Cases Checklist

Stop/search

***Osman v DPP* (1999)**
Police must comply with requirements of s 1 PACE or else their use of stop and search powers are unlawful

***Gillan and Quinton v UK* (2010)**
Powers to stop and search under s 44 Terrorism Act 2000 are too wide and breach human rights

Searching premises

***R v Longman* (1988)**
Police may use force or subterfuge to gain entry to premises under a warrant

***O'Loughlin v Chief Constable of Essex* (1998)**
Police should give reasons at point of entry unless it is impracticable

Powers of arrest

***Taylor v Chief Constable of Thames Valley Police* (2004)**
The person arrested must be told the reason for arrest in simple language

***Hayes v Chief Constable of Merseyside* (2011)**
The test for necessity has two parts,(1) honest belief by police officer, (2) that belief is objectively reasonable

Police Powers

Powers of detention

***R v Samuel* (1988)**
D must have access to a lawyer unless it is one of the situations set out in PACE where access can be delayed

***R v Aspinall* (1999)**
A vulnerable person must have an appropriate adult present during police interviews

***Charles v Crown Prosecution Service* (2009)**
D cannot normally be interviewed after he has been told he will be charged

Samples

***S and Marper v United Kingdom* (2009)**
Indefinite retention of DNA records is a breach of human rights

Exclusion of evidence

***R v Halliwell* (2012)**
Court has discretion to exclude evidence where PACE rules have been breached

9.1.2

Osman v DPP (1999) *The Times*, 28 September

DC

Key Facts

Police officers failed to give their names or station when using their powers of stop and search. This made the search unlawful.

O had resisted the search and been charged with assaulting a police officer in the execution of duty. Because the search was unlawful

O was entitled to use reasonable force.

Key Law

Police officers must comply with the requirements in s 1 Police and Criminal Evidence Act 1984 (PACE). If they do not, then the use of the power to stop and search is unlawful.

Key Link

Michaels v Highbury Corner Magistrates' Court [2009] EWHC 2928 (Admin).

Gillan v United Kingdom: Quinton v United Kingdom [2010] Crim LR 415

ECH

Key Facts

The applicants were, in separate instances, stopped and searched under the powers given by s 44 of the Terrorism Act 2000. They were then allowed to go on their way. They complained that s 44 breached their rights under various Articles of the European Convention on Human Rights. These were Articles 5 (right to liberty), 8 (right to respect for private life), 10 (freedom of expression) and 11 (freedom of assembly and association). The European Court of Human Rights held that s 44 breached Article 8. The court made no finding on any of the other Articles.

Key Law

Section 44 of the Terrorism Act 2000 breach Article 8 of the European Convention on Human Rights because it did not require the stop and search to be 'necessary' only 'expedient'. The discretion conferred on individual police officers was too broad. Also the fact that it was unnecessary for an officer to demonstrate the existence of any reasonable suspicion or have any subjective suspicion made the section too wide.

There was also a risk that such a widely framed power could be misused against demonstrators and protestors in breach of Articles 10 and/or 11.

9.2.3   *R v Longman* [1988] Crim LR 534

Key Facts

The police had a warrant to search specific premises. They knew that it would be difficult to gain entry, so they arranged for a plain clothes police woman to pretend to be delivering flowers from Interflora. When the door was opened to her, the police burst into the premises without immediately identifying themselves or showing the search warrant. Once in the property they showed the search warrant. It was held that the search was lawful.

Key Law

Where police have a warrant to search premises, they may use force or subterfuge to gain entry. The warrant should be shown to the occupiers as soon as reasonably practical.

9.2.3   *O'Loughlin v Chief Constable* [1998] 1 WLR 374   CA

Key Facts

Police forced their way into premises without explaining that it was in order to arrest O'Loughlin's wife for criminal damage. This made the entry unlawful and O'Loughlin was successful in claiming damages for injuries sustained when he tried to prevent the police from entering.

Key Law

Police should give reasons for entry unless the circumstances make it impracticable.

Key Judgment: Buxton LJ

'Freedom of the home from invasion is an interest of comparable importance to freedom from arrest and is deserving of a comparable degree of protection.'

9.2.3

Taylor v Chief Constable of Thames Valley Police [2004] EWCA Civ 1022

 CA

Key Facts

Taylor was a 10-year-old boy who had been throwing stones during an anti-vivisection demo. When he was present at a later protest he was identified by a police officer who arrested him saying: 'I am arresting you on suspicion of violent disorder on April 18, 1998 at Hillgrove Farm.' He sued for unlawful arrest, but the Court of Appeal held that it was a lawful arrest.

Key Law

The person arrested must be told in simple, non-technical language that they can understand the essential legal and factual grounds for their arrest.

9.2.3

Hayes v Chief Constable of Merseyside Police [2011] EWCA Civ 911

 CA

Key Facts

M had made a complaint to the police of assault and harassment by Hayes. The police phoned Hayes and arranged to meet him at a railway station. On his arrival at that meeting point he was arrested. D sued for false imprisonment on the basis that his arrest was not 'necessary' under s 24 PACE. The claim failed.

Key Law

Whether the arrest is necessary under s 24(5)(e) PACE (the arrest was necessary to allow the prompt and effective investigation of the offence) involves a two-stage test: (1) that the constable actually believed that arrest was necessary and (2) that objectively that belief was reasonable.

9.4.2

R v Samuel [1988] 2 All ER 135   CA

Key Facts

Samuel (S) was arrested on suspicion of robbery. His mother was informed of his arrest but when, during an interview by the police, S asked for a solicitor, the police refused him access to any lawyer. Shortly after, S confessed to the robbery. At his trial S contended that the evidence of his confession should be excluded as he had been refused access to legal advice. He was convicted. The conviction was quashed.

Key Law

PACE clearly sets out that access to legal advice can only be refused where the police believe that allowing consultation with a solicitor will lead to interference with, or harm to, the evidence or to other people, alert others or hinder the recovery of property.

Key Comment

This case stresses the importance of the right of access to legal advice.

9.4.3

R v Aspinall [1999] 2 Cr App Rep 115   CA

Key Facts

Aspinall (A) was arrested and taken to a police station. A police surgeon examined him and noted that he was a schizophrenic and on regular medication. The surgeon noted that A was anxious but lucid and probably fit to be interviewed. By the time of his interview A had been in custody some 13 hours. He initially requested a solicitor but changed his mind and stated he was anxious to get home to his family. Evidence of the interview was excluded, as it was held there should have been an appropriate adult present at the interview. Because of his mental illness A was a vulnerable person.

Key Law

Vulnerable people should have an appropriate adult present during police interviews.

9.4.3 *Charles v Crown Prosecution Service* [2009] EWHC 3521 (Admin) (DC)

Key Facts

D was found slumped over the steering wheel of a car and was arrested for being in charge of a vehicle whilst under the influence of drink or drugs. He took a breath test and was informed that he would be charged. After this he was interviewed. He was not informed of the offence for which the police were investigating him at the start of the interview. He was then charged with driving whilst under the influence of drink or drugs. The magistrates allowed the statement taken from him in the interview to be used in evidence. His conviction was quashed as there had been a breach of the Code of Practice in interviewing D.

Key Law

The Code of Practice under PACE stated that:

> 'a detainee may not be interviewed about an offence after they have been charged with, or informed that they may be prosecuted for it, unless the interview is necessary'.

These provisions are designed to protect a detainee and cannot be ignored.

9.4.3 *S v United Kingdom: Marper v United Kingdom* [2009] Crim LR 355 (ECHR)

Key Facts

S, aged 11, had been found not guilty of attempted robbery. M had been charged with harassment of his partner but the case had been dropped. Both had had DNA samples taken and their DNA profiles had been retained on the national police database. Both argued that the retention of their records on the database was contrary to their right to respect for private and family life under Article 8(1) of the European Convention on Human Rights. The European Court of Human Rights held that there was a breach of Article 8.

Key Law

The indefinite retention of DNA records of those who were not convicted of an offence was a breach of their right to respect for private life.

9.4.3 *R v Halliwell* [2012] EWCA Crim 2924   CA

Key Facts

The police interviewed Hallliwell away from the police station and ignored his repeated requests to be taken to a police station and to see a solicitor. The police also failed to caution him. His confession to murder obtained in this interview was excluded under s 78 PACE.

Key Law

The trial judge exercised his discretion under s 78 PACE to exclude the confession D gave in the interview as the failure to caution and the whole circumstances of the interview 'would have such an adverse effect on the fairness' of the proceedings that they ought not to be admitted.

Key Link

Richardson v The Chief Constable of West Midlands Police [2011] EWHC 773 (QB).

10 The Criminal Process and Courts

Crown Prosecution Service

- Prosecution of Offences Act 1985
- Decide what offence to change
- Can discontinue if
  a) insufficient evidence
  b) not in public interest
- Glidewell Report (1998) critical; led to changes

Bail

Police bail

Bail granted by court
- Bail Act 1976
- Presumption in favour of bail
- Can refuse if believe would fail to surrender or commit offence or interfere with witnesses

CRIMINAL PROCESS

Criminal courts

Crown Court
- indictable offences
- tried by judge and jury

Magistrates' Court
- summary offences
- may send triable either way to Crown Court
- tried by a District Judge or lay magistrates

Appeals

From Magistrates to:
- Queen's Bench Divisional Court by case stated

OR
- Crown Court

From Crown Court to:
- Court of Appeal
- further appeal to Supreme Court

▶ 10.1 The Crown Prosecution Service (CPS)

1   The CPS was set up by the Prosecution of Offences Act 1985 as an independent prosecuting body. The head of the CPS is the Director of Public Prosecutions.

2   The CPS may later decide to discontinue a case if on further investigation there is insufficient evidence or if it is not in the public interest to prosecute.

3   The Code for Crown Prosecutors sets out some common public interest factors considered.

4   Factors in favour of prosecution include:

- a weapon was used;
- the defendant was in a position of authority or trust;
- the offence was premeditated;
- the offence was carried out by a group;
- the defendant has relevant previous convictions.

5   Factors against prosecution include:

- the offence was committed as a result of a genuine mistake;
- the loss or harm is minor and arose from a single incident;
- the defendant is elderly or suffering from significant mental or physical illness.

6   The CPS is organized into 13 areas with a chief Crown Prosecutor for each area.

7   In the Magistrates' Court the CPS will be represented by a Crown Prosecutor (qualified lawyer) or by an Associate Prosecutor (non-lawyer).

8   In the Crown Court, the CPS can be represented by a Crown Prosecutor who has the relevant advocacy qualification or by an independent advocate. Advocacy rights in the Crown Court were given to employed CPS lawyers by the Access to Justice Act 1999.

▶ 10.2 Bail

Bail can be given by the police or it can be given by a court before which the defendant appears.

1   There is a presumption that bail should be granted (s 4 Bail Act 1976).

2   However, bail need not be granted where there are substantial grounds for believing that the accused would, if granted bail:

- fail to surrender to custody;
- commit an offence while on bail;
- interfere with witnesses or otherwise obstruct the course of justice.

3   The court can also refuse to grant bail if it is satisfied that the defendant should be kept in custody for his own protection.

4   Factors considered include:

- the nature and seriousness of the offence;
- the character, antecedents, associations and community ties of the defendant;
- the defendant's record of fulfilling his obligations under previous grants of bail;
- the strength of the evidence against the defendant.

10.2.1 Special cases

1   The presumption in favour of bail is removed where it appears that the defendant has committed a triable either way offence or an indictable offence while on bail.

2   For murder, attempted murder, manslaughter, rape or attempted rape where the defendant has already served a custodial sentence for such an offence, bail should only be granted in exceptional circumstances (s 56 Crime and Disorder Act 1998).

3   The prosecution may appeal against the grant of bail for any offence which carries a sentence of imprisonment.

10.2.2 Balancing conflicting interests

1   Individuals have a right to liberty (Human Rights Convention), but this right must be balanced against protection of the public. This balance must be considered when granting bail.

2   About 9% of those on bail commit further offences.

3   It is possible to use a curfew as a condition of bail, with electronic tagging to monitor those at risk of committing further offences.

4   About 9% of the prison population is in custody awaiting trial. Many of these are given non-custodial sentences or a very short prison sentence

which means their immediate release. These defendants are clearly not thought to be a danger to the public, but have had to stay in custody while awaiting trial.

10.3 Classification of offences

Summary offences	Triable either way offences	Indictable offences
Tried in Magistrates' Court Maximum sentence 6 months and/or £5,000 fine	Plea before venue • guilty plea – magistrates decide whether to hear case • not guilty plea – defendant has the right to elect trial by jury or stay in Magistrates' Court	First administrative hearing in Magistrates' Court Case then transferred to Crown Court • guilty plea – judge decides sentence • not guilty plea – jury decide verdict

The trial court is determined by the category of the offence being tried. There are three categories of offence. These are:

● summary – the least serious and can only be tried at a Magistrates' Court;

● triable either way – the middle range of offences and can be tried in either the Magistrates' Court or the Crown Court;

● indictable – the most serious offences and can only be tried at the Crown Court.

10.4 Magistrates' Court

10.4.1 Jurisdiction of the Magistrates' Court

1   Tries all summary offences and any offence triable either way where both the magistrates and the defendant agree to it being tried in the Magistrates' Courts.

2   These two categories account for about 97% of all criminal cases and in about 90% of these the defendants plead guilty.

3 The maximum sentence in the Magistrates' Courts is six months' imprisonment for one offence (12 months for two offences) and a fine of £5,000.

4 Conducts plea before venue hearings in respect of all triable either way offences. Any defendant who pleads guilty will then be dealt with in the Magistrates' Court.

5 Where a defendant pleads not guilty to a triable either way offence, a mode of trial hearing will then be held to decide whether the case should be tried in the Magistrates' Court or the Crown Court.

6 Deals with the first hearing of all indictable offences; these cases are then sent to the Crown Court.

7 Decides whether to grant arrest warrants or search warrants, and whether the defendant should be granted bail.

8 Youth Court hears cases involving those aged 10 to 17 inclusive.

9 The Magistrates' Court also has civil jurisdiction. This includes:

   - hearing appeals against a local authority's refusal to grant licences to pubs or other venues to sell alcohol;
   - enforcing demands for council tax;
   - hearing family cases;
   - proceedings under the Children Act 1989.

10.4.2 The Youth Court

1 Young offenders aged 10 to 17 inclusive are tried here. The exception is young offenders charged with very serious offences including murder, manslaughter, rape, or causing death by dangerous driving, who must be tried at the Crown Court. In addition, other serious offences (carrying a sentence of 14 years' imprisonment or more for an adult) may be tried in the Crown Court.

2 There must be three magistrates on the bench, with a mix of sexes, and the magistrates in the Youth Court have special training.

3 The procedure is less formal than in the adult court, with only authorised persons present.

4 A parent or guardian must be present where the offender is under 16, unless it would be unreasonable to require such attendance in the circumstances.

10.5 Appeals from the Magistrates' Court

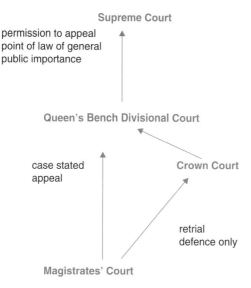

There are two different appeal routes.

1   Case stated appeal to the Queen's Bench Divisional Court (QBD).

   a) This is used where the appeal is on a point of law – the magistrates are asked to state a case (finding of facts). The QBD can quash the decision, confirm it or remit the case to the Magistrates' Court for a re-hearing.

   b) This route is available for both prosecution and defence.

   c) A further appeal is possible to the Supreme Court. This must be on a point of law of general public importance and the Supreme Court (or QBD) must give permission to appeal. This is only used a few times each year.

2   The Crown Court.

   a) This route is only available to the defendant. The appeal can be on sentence or conviction or both.

   b) The whole case is reheard at the Crown Court by a judge and two lay magistrates.

   c) There is no further appeal, unless a point of law is involved when the appeal then goes to the QBD as above.

▶ 10.6 The Crown Court

1   The Crown Court sits in about 90 centres.

2   Once a case has been transferred from the Magistrates' Court, a plea and directions hearing will be held to establish whether the plea is guilty or not guilty and to identify key issues for the trial.

3   If the defendant pleads guilty, the judge will decide the sentence.

4   If the defendant pleads not guilty, the trial is held before a judge and a jury of 12. The judge decides the law and the jury decides the facts. The jury decides whether the defendant is guilty or not guilty. This can be by a unanimous verdict or by a majority verdict (11 to 1 or 10 to 2).

▶ 10.7 Appeals from the Crown Court

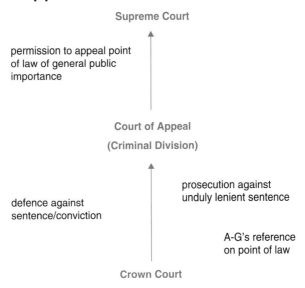

The defendant may appeal against conviction and/or sentence. The prosecution has limited rights of appeal against conviction and sentence.

10.7.1 Appeals by the defendant

1   The defendant may appeal against conviction and/or sentence to the Court of Appeal (Criminal Division). In all cases the defendant needs leave to appeal from the Court of Appeal, or the trial judge must grant a certificate that the case is fit for appeal.

2   The only ground for allowing an appeal against conviction is that the conviction is unsafe (s 2(1) Criminal Appeal Act 1968 as amended by the Criminal Appeal Act 1995).

3   If the Court of Appeal allows the defendant's appeal, it may order a retrial (s 7 Criminal Appeal Act 1968 as amended by the Criminal Justice Act 1988) or it may quash the conviction.

4   When hearing an appeal, the Court of Appeal has power to admit fresh evidence if it is necessary or expedient in the interests of justice (s 23(1) Criminal Appeal Act 1968).

10.7.2 Appeals by the prosecution

1   The prosecution may apply to the High Court for an order to quash an acquittal because of interference with a witness or the jury (s 54 Criminal Procedure and Investigations Act 1996).

2   Following an acquittal the Attorney-General may refer a point of law to the Court of Appeal (Criminal Division). This does not affect the acquittal; it merely states the law for future cases (s 36 Criminal Justice Act 1972).

3   The Criminal Justice Act 2003 allows the prosecution to appeal in respect of a ruling made by the trial judge on a point of law. The trial can be adjourned for the appeal to be decided. This will prevent defendants from being acquitted because the judge has made an error of law.

4   For serious offences such as murder and rape, the prosecution may apply to the Court of Appeal for an acquittal to be quashed and a re-trial to be ordered. This can only be done where there is new and compelling evidence that the defendant is guilty and it is in the interests of justice to hold a re-trial (ss 76–83 Criminal Justice Act 2003).

5   The Attorney-General may (with leave from the Court of Appeal) refer an unduly lenient sentence to the Court of Appeal for them to review the sentence (s 36 Criminal Justice Act 1988). The Court of Appeal can quash the original sentence and impose a more severe sentence.

10.7.3 Appeals to the Supreme Court

1   Both the prosecution and the defence have the right to appeal from the Court of Appeal (Criminal Division) to the Supreme Court.

2   In any case the Court of Appeal must have certified that the case involves a point of law of general public importance, and either the

Court of Appeal or the Supreme Court must give leave to appeal (s 33(2) Criminal Appeal Act 1968).

3   There is no appeal to the Supreme Court on sentence.

▶ 10.8 Miscarriages of justice

10.8.1 The Criminal Case Review Commission

1   The Criminal Case Review Commission (CCRC) was set up in 1997 under the Criminal Appeal Act 1995.

2   Prior to this the responsibility for referring possible miscarriages of justice back to the Court of Appeal lay with the Home Secretary. This was criticised as being too involved with the Executive and an ineffective method of dealing with possible miscarriages of justice.

3   The CCRC can investigate cases which were tried in the Crown Court or the Magistrates' Court. Where the case was tried in the Crown Court it may be referred to the Court of Appeal; where the trial was in the Magistrates' Court, the referral is to the Crown Court.

4   The CCRC can only refer a case if:

- an appeal has been decided or leave to appeal has been refused; and

- it considers there is a real possibility that the conviction (or sentence) would not be upheld (s 13 Criminal Appeal Act 1995).

Key Materials

10.1 Overriding objective

Rule 1.1 of the Criminal Procedure Rules states:

'(1) The overriding objective of this new code is that criminal cases be dealt with justly.

(2) Dealing with a criminal case justly includes:

    (a) acquitting the innocent and convicting the guilty;

    (b) dealing with the prosecution and the defence fairly;

    (c) recognising the rights of a defendant, particularly those under Article 6 of the European Convention on Human Rights;

(d) respecting the interests of witnesses, victims and jurors and keeping them informed of the progress of the case;

(e) dealing with the case efficiently and expeditiously;

(f) ensuring that appropriate information is available to the court when bail and sentence are considered; and

(g) dealing with the case in ways that take into account:

  (i) the gravity of the offence alleged,

  (ii) the complexity of what is in issue,

  (iii) the severity of the consequences for the defendant and others affected, and

  (iv) the needs of other cases.'

10.2 Active case management

Rule 3.2 of the Criminal Procedure Rules states:

'(1) The court must further the overriding objective by actively managing the case.

(2) Active case management includes:

  (a) the early identification of the real issues;

  (b) the early identification of the needs of witnesses;

  (c) achieving a certainty as to what must be done, by whom, and when, in particular by the early setting of a timetable for the progress of a case;

  (d) monitoring the progress of the case and compliance with directions;

  (e) ensuring that the evidence, whether disputed or not, is presented in the shortest and clearest way;

  (f) discouraging delay, dealing with as many aspects of the case as possible on the same occasion, and avoiding unnecessary hearings;

  (g) encouraging the participants to co-operate in the progression of the case; and

  (h) making use of technology.

(3) The court must manage the case by giving any direction appropriate to the needs of that case as early as possible.'

11 Sentencing

Sentencing aims

- Retribution
- Deterrence
- Protection/incapacitation
- Rehabilitation
- Reparation
- Denunciation

SENTENCING

Special powers for young offenders

- Detention and training orders
- Youth Rehabilitation order with requirements. eg
  a) attendance centre
  b) supervision
  c) action plan
  d) reparation
- Reprimands/warnings
- Referral to Youth Offending Panels

Sentences available

- Custodial
- Community order with requirements, eg:
  a) supervision
  b) unpaid work
  c) curfew
  d) drug treatment
- Fines
- Conditional/absolute discharge

1   A distinguishing feature of the criminal law is that there is the possibility of the State imposing a punishment on an offender. Hart's definition of 'punishment' is that it must:

- involve pain or other unpleasant consequences;

- be for an offence against legal rules;

- be intentionally administered by human beings other than the offender;

- be imposed and administered by an authority constituted by a legal system against which the offence is committed.

2   Before punishment is imposed, the sentencer should consider which aim(s) of sentencing to use, background factors (reports, etc) and the sentences available.

▶ 11.1 Aims of sentencing

1   These are concerned with the purpose or objective that the sentencer or policy-maker is seeking to achieve.

2   There are different sentencing aims that recognise the different needs of the offender, the victim and society. These needs may be in conflict.

3   Changes in penal policies can lead to one or more sentencing aims being preferred over others.

4   The purposes of sentencing are now set out in statute (s 142 Criminal Justice Act 2003). For offenders 18 and over the court must have regard to:

● the punishment of offenders;

● the reduction of crime (including its reduction by deterrence);

● the reform and rehabilitation of offenders;

● the protection of the public; and

● the making of reparation by offenders to persons affected by their offences.

5   For offenders under the age of 18, the purposes of sentencing are set out in s 142A Criminal Justice Act 2003. They are:

● the punishment of offenders;

● the reform and rehabilitation of offenders;

● the protection of the public; and

● the making of reparation by offenders to persons affected by their offences.

6   In addition the court must have regard *primarily* to the principal aim of the youth justice system to prevent offending and must also consider the welfare of the offender.

11.1.1 Punishment

1   Punishment is also referred to as retribution. It is thought of as being 'an eye for an eye and a tooth for a tooth', and society's revenge for the offence.

2   Its literal form is in the death penalty for murder: a life for a life. A literal interpretation is not practical for most offences and the aim is to 'let the punishment fit the crime'.

3   Retribution is based on blameworthiness, so a mentally ill offender should not be subjected to retribution.

4   Retribution is also based on proportionality or 'just desserts', so that the sentence reflects the seriousness of the offence. This concept is supported by the use of tariff sentences and guidelines issued by the Sentencing Guidelines Council.

5   Retribution can be seen in our sentencing legislation which states that a court must not pass a custodial sentence unless the offence was so serious that only a custodial sentence can be justified for the offence (s 152(2) Criminal Justice Act 2003 (CJA)).

11.1.2 Deterrence

1   There are two forms of deterrence:

   ● individual deterrence;

   ● general deterrence.

2   Individual deterrence is aimed at the particular offender. It aims to make the experience of punishment so unpleasant that the individual will not re-offend. Alternatively a threat (such as a suspended sentence) is used to deter.

3   General deterrence is aimed at discouraging others from committing that type of offence.

4   Deterrence is based on the assumption that potential offenders will consider the consequences of their actions. In fact, most offences are committed on the spur of the moment, so any deterrent effect is minimal.

5   Deterrence is not concerned with fairness or proportionality; the sentence imposed, especially for general deterrence, is likely to be harsher than the normal tariff for the offence.

11.1.3 Protection of society

1   This is usually achieved by incapacitation of the offender so that he or she cannot commit further offences. The ultimate example is the death penalty.

2   The sentence used to achieve incapacitation may be more severe than that needed for retribution. This conflict has been called 'deservedness versus dangerousness' (*von Hirsch*).

3   In our penal system a long custodial sentence is the usual method of incapacitation.

4   Section 225 of the Criminal Justice Act 2003 sets out that life imprisonment can be given where an offender has committed a serious violent or sexual offence and there is a significant risk of harm to the public from further offending.

5   There are other sentences which rely on incapacitation. For example, disqualification from driving; or disqualification from owning an animal for an offence of cruelty.

6   Electronic tagging gives a degree of incapacitation while allowing the offender to remain in the community.

11.1.4 Rehabilitation

1   This aims to reform the offender and so reduce the likelihood of future re-offending.

2   A sentence aimed at rehabilitation is considered an individualised sentence as opposed to the tariff sentences given under the retributive aim. Individualised sentences can lead to apparent inconsistency in sentencing.

3   It is now accepted that imprisonment has only limited rehabilitative effect.

4   The Criminal Justice Act 2003 provides for a community order to be made with requirements attached to it. The court can specify any requirements which it thinks will help in rehabilitating the offender. (The possible requirements are listed at 11.2.3.)

5   These requirements have been developed as studies of re-offending rates showed that those placed on probation with no additional requirements were almost as likely to re-offend as those given custodial sentences.

6   Rehabilitation is particularly important for young offenders to try to break the cycle of re-offending.

11.1.5 Reparation or restitution

1   There has been increasing concern that victims are not adequately considered when sentencing the offender.

2   Compensation orders are used instead of or in addition to the sentence imposed on the offender as reparation to the victim.

3   If the court does not make a compensation order when it has power to do so, then it must give reasons for not doing so (s 130 Powers of Criminal Courts (Sentencing) Act 2000 (PCC(S)A)).

4   Unpaid work requirements involve the offender doing a certain number of hours' work on community projects. This has an element of reparation to society at large.

5   An activity requirement in a community order can contain an element of reparation where the court thinks this is suitable.

6   A reparation order can be made where the offender is under 18. This can order reparation to the victim or the community at large (s 73 PCC(S)A).

11.1.6 Denunciation

1   Although denunciation is not referred to in the purposes of sentencing in the Criminal Justice Act 2003, theorists recognise it as an aim of sentencing.

2   This is expressing society's outrage at the offence committed.

3   It emphasises the criminality of the offence, but it goes beyond retribution in that society's expectations are also considered.

4   Denunciation is the main aim behind long prison sentences being imposed for offences of causing death by dangerous driving.

5   Failure by the courts to punish in accordance with society's expectations may lead to people taking action themselves, eg vigilantes.

▶ 11.2 Types of sentences

11.2.1 Custodial sentences

1   Murder carries a mandatory sentence of life imprisonment for offenders aged 18 and over. Offenders under 18 who are convicted of murder are detained at Her Majesty's pleasure (s 90 PCC(S)A). The minimum term to be served is governed by Schedule 22 of the Criminal Justice Act 2003.

2   For other offences a prison sentence up to the maximum for the particular offence can be imposed on offenders aged 18 and over. Offenders under 18 who are convicted of serious offences may be detained for a set period up to the maximum for the offence.

3   Under s 225 Criminal Justice Act 2003 a life sentence for public protection can be given to an offender who commits a serious violent or sexual
offence for which the maximum penalty is life.

4   Under s 227 Criminal Justice Act 2003 an offender who commits a less
serious violent or sexual offence can be given an extended sentence.
The period of extension is served on licence in the community. This
period can be up to five years for a violent offence and up to eight years
for a sexual offence.

5   A term of imprisonment for less than 12 months is known as 'custody
plus'. This is because the offender will serve part of the time in prison
and then the remainder on licence with requirements attached.

6   The Criminal Justice Act 2003 introduced the concept of intermittent
custody but this was abolished in 2007.

7   Offenders aged 18–20 may serve their sentence in a prison or Young
Offenders Institution (s 61 Criminal Justice and Court Services Act
2000).

8   Offenders aged 12–17 can be sentenced to a detention and training
order for a specified period of between four and 24 months.

11.2.2 Minimum sentences

1   Offenders convicted of a third offence of class A drug trafficking
must be sentenced to a minimum of seven years' imprisonment
(s 110 PCC(S)A).

2   Offenders convicted of a third offence of burglary must be sentenced to
a minimum of three years' imprisonment (s 111 PCC(S)A).

11.2.3 Community orders

1   The Government emphasis has been on extending the types of
community sentences available and on making them 'tougher' so that
they are not seen as a soft option.

2   Section 177(1) of the Criminal Justice Act 2003 allows a court to impose
on defendants aged 16 or over, as part of a community order, any one or
more of the following requirements:

a)   an unpaid work requirement;

b)   an activity requirement;

c)   a programme requirement;

d) a prohibited activity requirement;

e) a curfew requirement;

f) an exclusion requirement;

g) a residence requirement;

h) a mental health treatment requirement;

i) a drug rehabilitation requirement;

j) an alcohol treatment requirement;

k) a supervision requirement; and

l) in the case where the offender is aged under 25, an attendance centre requirement.

3   The court can only impose a mental health treatment requirement, a drug rehabilitation requirement or an alcohol treatment requirement where the defendant expresses his willingness to comply with the requirement.

▶ 11.3 Other powers of the court

1   A fine can be imposed for any offence. There is no limit to the amount which the Crown Court can fine an offender. The maximum fine in the Magistrates' Court is £5,000, except for health and safety offences where it is £20,000.

2   There are limits on the amount young offenders can be fined:

● 10–13 year olds: maximum £250;

● 14–17 year olds: maximum £1,000.

3   A conditional discharge may be given for a period of up to three years on the condition that during this time the offender does not re-offend (s 12 PCC(S)A).

4   An absolute discharge may be given. This has no conditions attached; the matter is at an end.

5   Disqualification from driving can be ordered for driving offences and also for non-driving offences, eg theft (s 146 PCC(S)A).

▶ 11.4 Additional powers in respect of young offenders (10–17)

1   A youth rehabilitation order can be made with various requirements.

2   The requirements under a youth rehabilitation order are similar to those for adults but also include a local authority residence requirement and an education requirement.

3   A reprimand or a warning may be given. These are not sentences imposed by a court. They are methods by which the police may deal with a young offender without taking the case to court.

4   Referral to a youth offender team must be ordered where an offender who has no previous convictions has pleaded guilty to an offence in court. Referral is also obligatory after a warning.

5   An offender's parent or guardian may be bound over for a period of up to three years to take proper care and exercise proper control of the offender.

6   A parenting order requiring parents to attend counselling or guidance sessions can be made when an offender under the age of 18 is convicted of an offence. The order is also available in civil proceedings where the court makes a child safety order (s 8 Crime and Disorder Act 1998).

▶ 11.5 Mentally ill offenders

1   In addition to the normal range of penalties there are special powers available to the court to deal with an offender who is mentally ill.

2   The main powers are:

- to add a requirement to a community order that the offender attends for treatment; or

- to make a hospital order to enable the offender to receive appropriate treatment as an in-patient; or

- where the offender is a danger to the community, to make a restriction order sending the offender to a secure hospital (s 41 Mental Health Act 1983).

▶ 11.6 Other factors in sentencing

11.6.1 Factors surrounding the offence

1   The level of seriousness of the offence within its type is important, eg the amount stolen, the seriousness of injuries inflicted, the type of weapon used.

2   Other factors that aggravate an offence include:

- premeditation;

- a vulnerable victim;

- an abuse of trust;
- being the ring leader;
- racial or religious hostility (s 145 CJA);
- hostility based on sexual orientation or disability (s 146 CJA).

3   Where the offender has pleaded not guilty, these facts will have been given as part of the evidence.

4   Where the offender has pleaded guilty, the facts of the case are outlined to the court by the prosecution. If the defendant does not agree with the prosecution's version, then a Newton hearing is held to establish the facts.

11.6.2 The offender's background

1   Previous convictions of the offender or any failure to respond to previous sentences may be taken into account in considering the seriousness of the offence.

2   Pre-sentence reports on the offender and his background may be available for the court.

3   The stage in the court proceedings at which the defendant pleaded guilty to the offence is considered.

4   The Sentencing Council guidelines include that where the defendant pleaded guilty at the first reasonable opportunity there should be a reduction of up to one third. The amount of reduction is on a sliding scale as shown in the diagram below.

5   If the evidence is overwhelming, then the reduction for a guilty plea is limited to 20%.

Stage in the proceedings

Proportionate reduction

12 The legal profession

LEGAL PROFESSION

SOLICITORS
Training

BARRISTERS
Training

Degree, if not in law then must do
Graduate Diploma in Law

- Legal Practice Course
- Training contract

- Bar Professional Training Course
- Pupillage

Role

- Private practice in solicitors' firm
- Wide variety of work
- Contracts, leases, wills conveyancing etc.

Role

- Self-employed in chambers
- Mostly court work
- Also write opinions and draft documents
- Direct access in civil cases only

May be employed in CPS, CDS, local authority,
etc or private commercial business

Advocacy rights

Advocacy certificate
(Courts and Legal
Services Act 1990)
Provision for full rights
(Access to Justice Act 1999)

Advocacy rights

Full rights

Supervision

Law Society

Supervision

Bar Council

Legal Ombudsman

▶ 12.1 Solicitors

12.1.1 Training

1   To become a solicitor it is usual to have a law degree which covers the seven core subjects of:

- contract law;
- law of torts;
- criminal law;
- land law;
- equity and trusts;
- constitutional and administrative law;
- European Union law.

If a student has a degree in another subject it is necessary to take the Graduate Diploma in Law.

1   The next stage is the one-year Legal Practice Course (LPC) or Graduate Diploma in Law (GDL), which includes training in skills such as client interviewing, negotiation and advocacy.

2   After passing this the student must then obtain a training contract. This can be with a firm of solicitors, or in an organisation such as the Crown Prosecution Service (CPS) or the legal department of a local authority. The training contract is for a period of two years and gives the trainee solicitor practical experience.

3   A 20-day Professional Skills Course must be completed during the training period.

4   After completing all the above the trainee will be admitted as a solicitor by the Law Society.

5   There is also a route for non-graduate mature students to qualify. This is by becoming a fellow of the Institute of Legal Executives (must be over 25 years, have passed the Professional Diploma in Law and the Professional Higher Diploma in Law and have worked in a solicitor 's office for at least five years). They must then take the LPC examinations.

12.1.2 Role

1   The majority of those who qualify as solicitors will work in private practice in a solicitor's firm.

2   Initially they will work as an assistant solicitor in a firm, but may eventually become a partner or set up on their own as a sole practitioner.

3   There is no maximum on the number of partners in a firm of solicitors. The size of firms varies from the sole practitioner to partnerships with over 100 partners and several hundred assistant solicitors.

4   The work of a solicitor will vary according to the type of firm. Small high street firms are likely to concentrate on family law, wills and probate, housing law, consumer law and criminal law. Large city firms specialise in business and commercial law.

5   Other careers are available as an employed lawyer in an organisation such as the CPS, Civil Service or local authority. Solicitors are also employed by private businesses as legal advisers.

12.1.3 Advocacy rights

1   Solicitors in private practice can also act as advocates. They have always had full advocacy rights in the Magistrates' Court and the County Court.

2   The Courts and Legal Services Act 1990 allowed them to apply for an advocacy certificate for rights in the higher courts, but only about 5% have applied for a certificate.

3   The Access to Justice Act 1999 provided that all solicitors will be given full rights of audience. The intention was to bring in new training requirements to ensure that newly qualified solicitors will automatically have advocacy rights but this has not yet happened.

4   Solicitors employed by the CPS may act as a prosecutor-advocate in any court for which they hold an advocacy qualification.

5   Solicitors employed by the Legal Services Commission may act as an advocate to represent members of the public in any court for which they hold an advocacy qualification.

6   Other employed solicitors only have rights of audience to represent their employer.

▶ 12.2 Barristers

12.2.1 Training

1   To qualify as a barrister it is usual to have a law degree. If a student has a degree in another subject then it is necessary to take the Graduate Diploma in Law.

2   Would-be barristers must then take the Bar Professional Training Course (BPTC), which places emphasis on practical skills of drafting pleadings and advocacy.

3   All students must also become a member of one of the four Inns of Court and must either dine at that Inn a set number of times or attend weekend courses run by the Inn.

4   After passing the BPTC and completing the necessary attendance at an Inn of Court, the person is called to the Bar and is officially qualified as a barrister. However, before they can appear in court they must do a 12-month period of pupillage, 'work-shadowing' a barrister.

12.2.2 Role

1   Barristers at the Bar are self-employed. They usually practise from chambers, sharing expenses of rent, secretarial staff, etc.

2   They are independent and can be briefed by any solicitor. In addition, in civil cases, they can be approached directly by the public.

3   The majority of barristers concentrate on advocacy and they have rights of audience in all courts. Their other work involves giving advice and opinions on points of law or potential cases and drafting papers for court.

4   Some barristers specialising in areas such as taxation or patent law will rarely appear in court.

5   Employed barristers can work for the CPS, government departments, local authorities or businesses. Employed barristers now retain their rights of audience though there are limits on whom they may represent.

▶ 12.3 Queen's Counsel

1   After being qualified for ten years a barrister or solicitor may apply to 'take silk' and become a Queen's Counsel (QC).

2   Selection of who should become a QC is now made by an independent selection panel.

3   Lawyers apply to become QCs. They have to pay a fee. They are interviewed by members of the panel. Applicants provide references (these can include references from clients).

4   The panel then recommends those who should be appointed to the Lord Chancellor.

▶ 12.4 Para-legals

12.4.1 Legal executives

1 To become a Fellow of the Institute of Legal Executives (ILEX) it is necessary to be over 25 years of age, to have passed Professional Diploma in Law and the Professional Higher Diploma in Law and to have worked in a solicitor's firm (or other comparable employment, eg CPS) for at least five years.

2 Legal executives work in solicitors' firms and deal with the more straightforward cases.

3 They have limited rights of audience in the County Court to make unopposed applications.

12.4.2 Licensed conveyancers

1 These specialise in the conveyancing of property.

2 Complaints about licensed conveyancers are dealt with by the Legal Ombudsman.

▶ 12.5 Regulation of the legal professions

12.5.1 The Law Society

1 This is the governing body of solicitors.

2 It is a regulatory body that can set rules and discipline solicitors.

3 It also acts as the representative of the interests of solicitors.

4 Complaints by clients about solicitors are handled by the Office for Legal Complaints through the Legal Ombudsman.

5 Issues of professional misconduct are heard by the Solicitors Regulatory Authority. The Solicitors Disciplinary Council has the power to strike off solicitors.

12.5.2 The Bar Council

1 This is the governing body of barristers.

2 As with the Law Society, it has both regulatory and representative functions.

3   Complaints by clients about barristers are handled by the Office for Legal Complaints through the Legal Ombudsman.

4   The Bar Standards Board will hear allegations of breach of the Bar's Code of Conduct and the Senate of the Inns of Court has the power to disbar a barrister.

12.5.3 Suing a lawyer

1   There is a contract between a solicitor and client. So, if there is a breach of contract, the client has the right to sue the solicitor. There is no contract between a client and their barrister.

2   It is possible for a client to sue both solicitors and barristers for negligence. In some cases where the negligence has caused loss to a third person, that person may be able to sue (*Ross v Caunters* (1979), *White v Jones* (1995)).

3   It used not to be possible to sue either a barrister or a solicitor for negligent advocacy (*Rondel v Worsley* (1969), *Saif Ali v Sydney Mitchell and Co* (1980)). However, this rule was changed in the case of *Hall v Simons* (2000) and it is now possible to sue for negligent advocacy.

▶ 12.6 Legal Services Act 2007

12.6.1 Regulation of the legal profession

1   The Act created the Legal Services Board (LSB).

2   It consists of a Chairman and seven to ten members. The majority of members must be non-lawyers

3   The role of the Board is to have independent oversight regulation of the legal profession.

4   Primary responsibility for regulation rests with the Law Society and Bar Council and the LSB should only interfere when their actions are palpably unreasonable.

12.6.2 Alternative business structures (ABSs)

1   The Act allows legal businesses to:
   ● include lawyers and non-lawyers;
   ● include barristers and solicitors;

- be owned by non-lawyers;
- be operated as companies.

2 ABSs were introduced in 2011.

3 In deciding on giving licences to operate ABSs, access to justice must be properly considered.

Key Cases Checklist

Solicitors' duty of care

***Ross v Caunters* (1979)**
Solicitors can be liable to third parties where their negligence causes a foreseeable loss

***White v Jones* (1995)**
A solicitor owes a duty of care to a third party (eg a beneficiary)

The Legal Profession

Advocates' immunity

***Hall, Arthur J S, & Co v Simons* (2000)**
Advocates are no longer immune from claims in negligence

12.5.3   ***Ross v Caunters* [1979] 3 WLR 605**   HL

Key Facts

Solicitors prepared a will for a client and sent it to him for it to be signed and witnessed. They failed to warn him that the will should not be witnessed by the spouse of any beneficiary. One of the witnesses was the husband of a beneficiary. As a result she was not able to inherit under the will. She sued the solicitors for the loss suffered. The solicitors claimed that they only had a duty of care to the testator. The judge held that they owed a duty of care to the beneficiary.

Key Law

Solicitors can be liable to a third party, where their negligence causes that third party a foreseeable loss.

Key Judgment: Megarry V-C

'If one examines the facts of the case before me to discover whether the three-fold elements of the tort of negligence exist, a simple answer would be on the following lines. First, the solicitors owed a duty of care to the plaintiff since she was someone within their direct contemplation as a person so closely and directly affected by their acts and omissions in carrying out their client's instructions to provide her with a share of his residue that they could reasonably foresee that she would be likely to be injured by those acts and omissions. Second, there has undoubtedly been a breach of that duty of care; and third, the plaintiff has clearly suffered loss as a direct result of that breach of duty.'

Key Comment

It had previously been accepted that solicitors owed a duty of care to their client, but this case extended the scope of a solicitors' duty of care. This principle was approved by the House of Lords in *White v Jones* (1995) (see below).

12.5.3   ### *White v Jones* [1995] 1 All ER 691   HL

Key Facts

A solicitor was instructed by a client to change the client's will so that his daughters (to whom he had previously left nothing) would receive £9,000 each. The solicitor delayed and did not do anything for some months, so that the client died without the change being made. The old will was effective and the daughters did not receive anything under it. They were successful in claiming £9,000 each from the solicitor.

Key Law

A solicitor owes a duty of care to an intended beneficiary of a will when instructed by the testator to draw up the will.

12.5.3

Hall, Arthur J S & Co v Simons [2000] 3 All ER 673

(HL)

Key Facts

Three cases were joined on appeal. In all three cases there was a claim against a firm of solicitors for negligence and, in each, the firm relied on the rule, established in *Rondel v Worsley* (1969) that an advocate was immune from any claim in negligence. The House of Lords held that it was no longer in the public interest that advocates should be immune from claims.

Key Law

The decision in *Rondel v Worsley* was overruled. Advocates are no longer immune from claims in negligence.

Key Comment

The House of Lords considered the four points given in *Rondel v Worsley* as reasons for immunity. These were:

1. Advocate's divided loyalty: an advocate owes a duty to the court as well as to his client. The Law Lords stated that removing immunity was unlikely to have a significantly adverse effect on any duty owed to the court.

2. Cab rank principle: this is a rule that barristers are obliged to accept any case, provided it is in the area of law in which they practise. It had been argued that a barrister who had to accept any client would be unfairly exposed to vexatious claims. The Law Lords stated that such a claim did not have any real substance.

3. The witness analogy: it is well established that a witness is absolutely immune from liability for anything he says in court. However, a witness does not owe anyone a duty of care. He only has a duty to tell the truth. An advocate has a duty of care to his client.

4. Protraction of litigation: allowing a claim for negligent advocacy could, in effect, lead to a re-trial of the original case. The Law Lords accepted that there might be a risk of this happening, but pointed out that, in criminal cases, starting a civil action for negligence while there was still an appeal route open to the defendant would normally be an abuse of process. Once a conviction had been set aside, then there could be no public policy objection to a claim for negligence. In civil cases, the outcome was only of interest to the parties and so there was no public interest objection to a subsequent finding that, but for the negligence of his advocate, the losing party would have won.

13 The Judiciary

Superior judges

- Justices of the Supreme Court
- Lords Justices of Appeal
- High Court Judges
- Selection by Judicial Appointments Commission
- Appointed by monarch
- Security of tenure
- Largely white/male

Inferior judges

- District Judges
- Recorders
- Circuit Judges
- Posts advertised: applicants interviewed
- Appointment by monarch
- Increasing number of women and ethnic minorities

JUDICIARY

Independence of judiciary

- Separation of powers
- Immunity from suit
- Superior judges have security of tenure

But

- 'Conservative'
- White/male dominated
- Public school/Oxbridge dominated

Lord Chancellor

- Appointed by Prime Minister
- Role is in conflict with separation of powers
- Involvement in judicial appointments
- Responsible for courts and funding
- Responsible for many other public offices

Judges can be divided into two main types: inferior judges and superior judges. These categories affect the way judges are appointed, the courts they sit in and the way they can be dismissed.

▶ 13.1 Appointment

1 The professional qualifications needed to become a judge are set out in the Courts and Legal Services Act 1990 as amended by the Tribunals, Court and Enforcement Act 2007. To be appointed it is necessary to have a legal qualification and to have gained experience in the law for a certain period of time.

2 Up to 2005 the Lord Chancellor played a major part in selecting and recommending judges for appointment.

3 Since 2005 the selection of judges has been by the Judicial Appointments Commission.

13.1.1 The Judicial Appointments Commission

1 This was set up under the Constitutional Reform Act 2005.

2 There are 15 members of this Commission:
- 6 lay members;
- 5 judges – 3 of these to be from the Court of Appeal or High Court plus 1 circuit judge and 1 district judge or equivalent;
- 1 barrister, 1 solicitor, 1 magistrate and 1 tribunal member.

3 All judicial vacancies are advertised. Candidates must apply.

4 All selection is based entirely on merit.

5 The Commission will recommend to the Lord Chancellor who should be appointed.

6 The Lord Chancellor has limited powers in relation to each recommendation for appointment. He is able to reject a candidate once or ask the Commission to reconsider once and, in doing so, he must provide reasons. The Courts and Crime Act 2013 has removed this power in respect of inferior judges.

7 Once the Lord Chancellor has accepted the recommendations, all judges are then appointed by the Monarch.

13.1.2 Inferior judges

1 District Judges sit in the County Court and Magistrates' Court. They:
- must be qualified as a barrister or solicitor and have gained experience in law for at least five years or to have been a Deputy District Judge;

- Deputy District Judges can also be appointed from those qualified as an ILEX Fellow.

2   Recorders are part-time judges who can sit in the County Court and the Crown Court. They:

- must be qualified as a barrister or solicitor and have gained experience in law for at least seven years;
- are appointed for a renewable period of five years;
- must sit for at least 15–30 days per year.

3   Circuit Judges are full-time judges who sit in the County Court and/or Crown Court. They:

- must be qualified as a barrister or solicitor and have gained experience in law for at least seven years or have been a Recorder or District Judge.

13.1.3 Superior judges

1   High Court Judges or Puisne Judges sit in the High Court. They will be appointed to one of the three divisions (Queen's Bench, Chancery or Family). They:

- must be qualified as a barrister or solicitor and have gained experience in law for at least seven years or have been a Circuit Judge for at least two years;
- will usually have sat as a Deputy High Court judge before being appointed.

2   Lords Justices of Appeal sit in the Court of Appeal and must be qualified as a barrister or solicitor and have gained experience in law for at least seven years or be an existing High Court Judge.

3   Justices of the Supreme Court must have been qualified to appear in senior courts for at least 15 years or have held high judicial office in England and Wales or Scotland or Northern Ireland for at least two years.

13.1.4 Comments on the appointment system

1   Reform of the old system was needed as it was felt that the Lord Chancellor had too much influence in appointments.

2   The old system had an emphasis on the 'old boy' network, with the use of secret soundings.

3   There were only a small number of women judges, especially in the High Court and above. It was not until 2004 that the first woman judge was appointed to the House of Lords and is now in the Supreme Court.

4   The Judicial Appointments Commission is independent of the Government. They have taken positive steps to encourage applications from women and ethnic minority lawyers.

5   Under the new appointments system there are many more women and ethnic minority judges being appointed.

6   Women now make up about 30% of appointments in the lower levels of the judiciary, and about 12% in the High Court and above.

7   Overall there about 4% of ethnic minority judges. However, representation at the higher levels is still much lower.

▶ 13.2 Training

1   This is organised by the Judicial College.

2   For most new judges there is a short residential course (three or four days).

3   New Recorders also have to visit two penal establishments and sit in on trials at a Crown Court.

4   Most judges will attend a continuation seminar once every three years.

5   There are additional special training schemes for areas of law such as the Human Rights Act 1998.

6   Part-time judges are subject to appraisal schemes.

7   There is criticism that the training of judges is inadequate, in particular that the initial course for Recorders is too short, as lawyers who are not criminal law practitioners will be expected to sit on criminal cases.

▶ 13.3 Removal

1   It is seen as important that judges should be independent, so they must be protected from removal at the whim of the Government.

2   As a result, superior judges have security of tenure that dates back to the Act of Settlement 1701. They can only be removed by the Monarch following a petition presented by both Houses of Parliament.

3   The Lord Chancellor can, after consultation with the Lord Chief Justice, declare vacant the office of any judge who, through ill-health, is incapable of carrying out his work and of taking the decision to resign.

4   Inferior judges can be dismissed by the Lord Chancellor for incapacity or misbehaviour (s 17(4) Courts Act 1971), but only if the Lord Chief Justice consents to the dismissal.

▶ 13.4 Independence of the Judiciary

13.4.1 Doctrine of the separation of powers

1   This doctrine was first put forward by Montesquieu in the eighteenth century.

2   The theory is that the three primary functions of the State (Legislature, Executive and Judiciary) must be kept separate in order to safeguard the rights of citizens.

3   In our Government the Legislature is Parliament, the Executive is the Cabinet and the Judiciary is the judges.

4   There is an overlap of the Legislature and Executive as the Cabinet are also members of Parliament.

5   The Lord Chancellor's role goes across all three arms of State.

6   The judges on the Judicial Committee of the House of Lords used to sit in the House of Lords in a legislative capacity. However, this ceased when the Judicial Committee of the House of Lords was replaced by the Supreme Court.

13.4.2 The Judiciary

1   The Lord Chancellor is appointed by the Prime Minister and holds office only while the Prime Minister wishes.

2   The Lord Chancellor still plays a small role in judicial appointments. This is contrary to the doctrine of separation of powers, but this is being further limited.

3   Section 3 of the Constitutional Reform Act 2005 guarantees the principle of judicial independence. It states that the Lord Chancellor and other government ministers must uphold the continued independence of the judiciary.

13.4.3 Protection of judicial independence

1   Judges have immunity from being sued for anything they do in the course of their judicial duties (*Sirros v Moore* (1975)).

2   By convention, individual judges are not criticised during parliamentary debates.

3   Judicial salaries are paid from the Consolidated Fund so that payment is made without the need for parliamentary authorisation.

4   The security of tenure of superior judges protects them from the threat of removal by the Government.

13.4.4 Bias

1   Judges are viewed as too pro-establishment and conservative with a small 'c'. Professor Griffiths cites cases such as *Attorney-General v Guardian Newspapers Ltd* (1987) and *R v Secretary of State for the Home Office, ex parte Brind* (1991) to support this view.

2   Natural justice demands that no man be a judge in his own cause. In addition, a judge who is involved, whether personally or as a director of a company, in promoting the same causes as one of the parties to the action, is automatically disqualified from hearing the case (In *Re Pinochet Ugarte* (1999)).

3   The test for bias on the material circumstances of a judge's involvement is an objective test, ie whether or not the fair-minded observer would consider that there was a real danger of bias (*Director General of Fair Trading v The Proprietary Association of Great Britain* (2001), *Lawal v Northern Spirit Ltd* (2003)).

▶ 13.5 The Lord Chancellor's role

1   The Lord Chancellor is appointed by the Prime Minister and can be dismissed by him at any time. The Lord Chancellor will change with a change of Government.

2   The Lord Chancellor is involved in all three arms of State. He is:

- a member of Parliament (can sit in either House of Commons of House of Lords);

- a member of the Cabinet (the executive);

- involved in the appointment of the judiciary.

3   Under the Constitutional Reform Act 2005, the Lord Chancellor no longer needs to be a lawyer.

4   The Constitutional Reform Act 2005 also provides that the Lord Chancellor can be a member of the House of Lords or the House of Commons. In 2007 Jack Straw became the first Lord Chancellor to sit in the House of Commons.

5   The Lord Chancellor is also Minister of Justice. This Ministry was created in 2007 and has responsibility for a large number of justice areas including the courts, tribunals, the Community Legal Service, prisons and the probation service.

Key Cases Checklist

Independence of the judiciary

R v Bow Street Magistrates, ex p Pinochet Ugarte (No 2) (1999)
A judge should disclose his position or stand down if he has a close connection to any party or connected organisation

DirectorGeneral of Fair Trading v The Proprietary Association of Great Britain (2001)
The test for bias of the tribunal is whether a fair-minded observer would conclude that there was a real possibility of bias

Lawal v Northern Spirit Ltd (2003)
An advocate who has previously sat as a judge with a panel of lay members must not appear in frontof those same lay members in anothercase

13.4.4   *R v Bow Street Magistrates, ex p Pinochet Ugarte (No 2)* [1999] 1 All ER 577   HL

Key Facts

An extradition warrant was issued from Spain for General Pinochet, the former President of Chile. It alleged his complicity in crimes of murder, torture and conspiracy to murder which occurred in Chile while he was President. The English courts had to decide whether General Pinochet could rely on immunity as head of state at the time of the alleged crimes.

The House of Lords, on a three to two majority, rejected his right to claim immunity. Lord Hoffman was one of the majority but did not give reasons for his decision. Following the ruling, it was realised that Lord Hoffman was an unpaid director of the charitable trust run by Amnesty International. This was important because Amnesty had been granted leave to intervene in the proceedings and had made submissions to the Lords supporting the extradition.

The Law Lords set aside the decision on the basis that Lord Hoffman's involvement with Amnesty had invalidated the hearing.

Key Law

A judge should disclose his position or stand down if he has a close connection and an active role with a charity or other organisation involved in the litigation.

13.4.4

Director General of Fair Trading v The Proprietary Association of Great Britain [2001] 1 WLR 700

Key Facts

A case was being heard before the Restrictive Practices Court with lay members on the panel. Part way through the case one lay member disclosed that, since the start of the case, she had applied for a job with one of the main witnesses for one of the parties to the case. The respondents argued that such behaviour must imply bias on her part and that the whole panel should stand down. The Court of Appeal upheld this argument.

Key Law

The test set out by the House of Lords in *R v Gough* (1993) should be refined in the light of the implementation of the Human Rights Act 1998. The test should now be whether a fair-minded observer would conclude that there was a real possibility of bias.

Key Comment

The test is in line with decisions by the European Court of Human Rights. The test in *R v Gough* was a subjective one on the part of the court. The new test is an objective one where the matter is considered from the perspective of a fair-minded observer.

| 13.4.4 | *Lawal v Northern Spirit Ltd* [2003] UKHL 35 | HL |

Key Facts

A QC appeared in front of the Employment Appeal Tribunal acting for D who was the employer of the claimant. The QC had previously sat as a part-time judge in the Employment Appeal Tribunal and one of the lay members in the present case had been on the panel with the QC. The claim was dismissed but on appeal to the House of Lords, they held that the practice of advocates, who were part-time judges, subsequently appearing in front of lay members of the tribunal with whom they had sat should be discontinued as it tended to undermine public confidence.

Key Law

The principle to be applied was whether a fair minded and informed observer would conclude that there was a real possibility of bias.

14 Lay magistrates

Role in criminal cases

- try all summary offences
- sentence those who are guilty
- deal with mode of trial hearings for all triable either way offences
- deal with first hearing of indictable offences
- hear applications for bail
- issue arrest and search warrants
- sit in Youth Court

Civil work

- licensing appeals
- enforce council tax
- family cases

Qualifications / Appointment

- 18–65 on appointment
- Can sit until 70
- Live or work in or near area
- Sit at least 26 times a year
- Appointed by Lord Chancellor on recommendation of Local Advisory Committee

Lay Magistrates

Composition

- Just over 50% female
- 8% ethnic minority
- disabled magistrates encouraged

BUT

- middle class over-represented
- 'middle-aged' only 4% under 40

Advantages

- involvement of local lay people
- 3 magistrates gives a balanced view
- cheap
- improved training

Disadvantages

- high conviction rate
- not a cross-section of society
- inconsistency in sentencing and granting bail
- lack legal knowledge
- may rely too heavily on clerk

▶ 14.1 Qualifications

1   On appointment a person must be between 18 and 65 years of age. Since 2004 there has been a policy of appointing some younger magistrates, in their twenties or teens, where suitable.

2   They must live or work in or near the justice area to which they are appointed.

3   Those with a criminal conviction, undischarged bankrupts, members of the forces, police officers and traffic wardens are not eligible.

4   In 1998 the Lord Chancellor set out six key qualities which candidates should have. These are:

- good character;
- understanding and communication;
- social awareness;
- maturity and sound temperament;
- sound judgement;
- commitment and reliability.

Those appointed must be prepared to sit at least 26 times (and preferably 35 times) per year.

▶ 14.2 Appointment

1   Lay magistrates are appointed by the Lord Chancellor on behalf of the Queen.

2   The Lord Chancellor relies on recommendations made to him by local advisory committees.

3   The advisory committees can advertise for vacancies for lay magistrates. Local people can apply.

4   The local committees interview candidates and recommend suitable people to the Lord Chancellor.

5   In putting forward names the committee must also consider the composition of the local Bench in terms of gender, ethnic origin, occupation and political views. The aim is to keep as good a balance as possible of different types of people.

6   Employers are obliged to give employees time off to sit as lay magistrates (s 50 Employment Rights Act 1996).

▶ 14.3 Composition of the Bench

1   Despite the efforts at getting a good mix of people as lay magistrates, there is still a feeling that magistrates are 'middle-class, middle-aged and middle-minded' as the middle classes are over-represented.

2   Women are well represented, making up just over half of all lay magistrates.

3   Ethnic minorities used to be under-represented, but over the past few years more have been appointed and they now make up 8% of the magistracy.

4   There has been an effort to recruit disabled people to the Bench and the first blind magistrates were appointed in 1998.

5   Only 4% of lay magistrates are under the age of 40.

▶ 14.4 Training

1   Under the Lay Magistrates National Training Initiative, newly appointed magistrates have to achieve three basic competencies. These are:

- managing yourself – focusing on some of the basic aspects of self-management in relation to preparing for court, conduct in court and ongoing learning;

- working as a member of a team – focusing on the team aspect of decision-making in the Magistrates' Court;

- making judicial decisions – focusing on impartial and structured decision-making.

2   Each new magistrate keeps a Personal Development Log of their progress and has a mentor (an experienced magistrate) to assist them.

3   During the first two years of the new magistrate sitting in court, between 8 and 11 of the sessions will be mentored. In the same period the magistrate is also expected to attend about seven training sessions.

4   Appraisals are held to check whether magistrates have acquired the competencies.

5   This scheme involves practical training 'on the job'. It answers the criticisms of the old system where there was no check on whether magistrates had actually benefited from training sessions they attended.

▶ 14.5 Retirement and removal

1   Lay magistrates cannot sit on the Bench to hear cases after the age of 70, but are placed on the supplemental list.

2   Section 11 of the Courts Act 2003 gives the Lord Chancellor power to remove a lay justice for the following reasons:

- incapacity or misbehaviour;

- a persistent failure to meet such standards of competence as are prescribed by a direction given by the Lord Chancellor; or

- where the Lord Chancellor is satisfied that the lay justice is declining or neglecting to take a proper part in the exercise of his functions as a justice of the peace.

3   About ten lay magistrates are removed from office each year.

▶ 14.6 Role

1   Two or three lay magistrates sit together to form a Bench. They have wide powers over criminal cases. They have jurisdiction to:

- try all summary offences;
- sentence those who are guilty (the maximum sentence is six months' imprisonment – 12 months for two offences);
- deal with mode of trial hearings for all triable either way offences, and try those which it is decided should be dealt with in the Magistrates' Court;
- deal with the first hearing of all indictable offences and then transfer those cases to the Crown Court;
- hear applications for bail;
- issue arrest and search warrants.

2   Specially trained lay magistrates also sit in the Youth Court.

3   Lay magistrates also have jurisdiction to deal with the following civil matters:

- licensing appeals;
- enforcing demands for council tax;
- family cases.

4   Magistrates must act without bias and must make sure that justice is seen to be done (*R v Sussex Justices, ex p McCarthy* (1924)).

5   Each Bench is assisted by a Magistrates' Clerk who guides the magistrates on questions of law, practice and procedure.

6   The clerk must not take part in any decision-making (*R v Eccles Justices, ex p Fitzpatrick* (1989)). Any advice given should be given in open court (Practice Direction (2000)).

▶ 14.7 Advantages

1   There is involvement of lay people with local knowledge.

2   Having three magistrates on a panel is likely to give a balanced view.

3   Magistrates come from a greater cross-section of society than professional judges.

4   As they are only paid expenses, the system is cheaper than using professional judges.

5   Improved training and appraisal should improve the quality of the Bench.

▶ 14.8 Disadvantages

1   There is a much higher conviction rate in the Magistrates' Court than in the Crown Court. This leads to allegations of bias in favour of the police and prosecution.

2   There is not a balanced cross-section of society as the middle classes are over-represented on the Bench.

3   There is inconsistency in sentencing.

4   There is inconsistency in granting of bail.

5   Lay magistrates lack legal knowledge and may rely too heavily on the clerk.

Key Cases Checklist

No bias

***R v Sussex Justices, ex p McCarthy* (1924)**
There must not be even a suspicion that there has been an improper interference with the course of justice

Lay Magistrates

Role of the clerk

***R v Eccles Justices, ex p Fitzpatrick* (1989)**
A clerk should not retire with justices as a matter of course

***Practice Direction* (2000)**
Justices should seek the advice of the clerk in open court

14.6   *R v Sussex Justices, ex p McCarthy* [1924] 1 KB 256

Key Facts

Following a road traffic accident. McCarthy (M) was summonsed for dangerous driving. At the end of the case, when the magistrates retired to consider their verdict, the clerk of the court went with them. M was found guilty. His lawyers then discovered that the clerk was a partner in a firm of solicitors that was acting in a civil claim for a person who had been injured in the accident. There was no evidence that the clerk had in any way influenced the decision, but M's lawyers successfully applied to the Divisional Court for the conviction to be quashed.

Key Law

Nothing should be done which creates even a suspicion that there has been an improper interference with the course of justice.

Key Judgment: Lord Hewart CJ

'It is of fundamental importance that justice should not only be done but manifestly and undoubtedly be seen to be done.'

14.6   *R v Eccles Justices, ex p Fitzpatrick* (1989) 89 Cr App Rep 324

Key Facts

Fitzpatrick (F) was charged with burglary. He had elected summary trial and pleaded not guilty. He then sought to change his plea. During the hearing for this, the clerk of the court took an active role and retired with the magistrates when they considered the request. F was allowed to change his plea and the magistrates then heard mitigation in respect of sentencing. When they retired to consider the sentence, they asked the clerk to retire with them. He did so and remained with them for most of the time. The magistrate decided to commit F to the Crown Court for sentence. The Divisional Court quashed this decision and sent the case back to the Magistrates' court to be reheard by a new bench with a different clerk.

Key Facts

(1) Any request to the clerk to accompany the justices when they retire to consider a case should be made clearly by the magistrates and in open court.

(2) A clerk should not retire with justices as a matter of course.

Key Comment

With the implementation of the Human Rights Act 1998, this point has now been made even clearer in the following Practice Direction.

14.6

Practice Direction [2000] 4 All ER 895

Para 8

'At any time justices are entitled to receive advice to assist them in discharging their responsibilities. If they are in doubt as to the evidence which has been given, they should seek the aid of their legal adviser, referring to his/her notes as appropriate. This should normally be done in open court. Where the justices request their adviser to join them in the retiring room, this request should be made in the presence of the parties in court. Any legal advice given to the justices other than in open court should be clearly stated to be provisional and the adviser should subsequently repeat the substance of the advice in open court and give the parties an opportunity to make any representations they wish on that professional advice. The legal adviser should then state in open court whether the professional advice is confirmed or, if it is varied, the nature of the variation.'

15 Juries

Use of juries

- main use is for criminal trials in the Crown Court
- limited use in High Court and County Court for cases of:
  - defamation
  - false imprisonment
  - malicious prosecution
  - case involving fraud
- coroners' Courts to inquire into deaths involving the police and some accidents

Jury qualifications

- age between 18 and 70
- be registered to vote
- reside in UK for at least 5 years since 13th birthday

Disqualifcation

- disqualified for life for custodial sentence of 5 years or more
- disqualified for 10 years for any other custodial or suspended sentence or community order
- disqualified while on bail

Juries

Selection of Jury

- at random from electoral roll
- can be vetted for criminal records *R v Mason* (1980)
- in exceptional cases, eg terrorism, there can be vetting of background and political views
- can be challenged for cause at court
- prosecution can 'stand by' jurors

Advantages of Jury

- public involvement in trial
- public confidence
- democratic
- panel of 12 should avoid individual bias
- can come to 'just' verdict

Disadvantages of Jury

- verdict reached in secret
- may use unsuitable means of reaching verdict *R v Young* (1995)
- may be racially biased *Sander v UK* (2000)
- may not understand complicated cases
- compulsory nature of jury service is unpopular
- jurors can be 'nobbled'
- makes cases longer and more expensive

▶ 15.1 Use of juries

1   Juries are used in criminal cases in the Crown Court where the defendant pleads not guilty. It is only in exceptional cases where a jury has been 'nobbled' in an earlier trial that there can be a trial by judge alone in the Crown Court (*R v Twomey and others* (2009), *KS v R* (2010)).

2   There is limited use of juries in civil cases in the High Court and County Court. The only civil cases in which there is a right to jury trial are defamation, false imprisonment, malicious prosecution and fraud. Cases of personal injury should not be tried by jury (*Ward v James* (1966), *Hodges v Harland & Wolff* (1965), *H v Ministry of Defence* (1991), *Goldsmith v Pressdram Ltd* (1987)). Nor should a jury be used just because exemplary damages are claimed (*Racz v Home Office* (1994)).

3   Juries are used in the Coroners' Court to inquire into deaths occurring in or where a police officer is involved or which occurred in certain accidents.

▶ 15.2 Jury qualifications

1   The basic qualifications are laid down by the Juries Act 1974. These are that to serve on a jury a person must:

   ● be aged between 18 and 70;

   ● be registered as a parliamentary or local government elector;

   ● have been resident in the UK for at least five years since their thirteenth birthday.

2   In addition, people are disqualified from jury service if they:

   ● have been sentenced to life imprisonment or a custodial sentence of five years or more;

   ● have served any other custodial sentence or received a suspended prison sentence within the last ten years;

   ● have been subject to a community order within the last ten years;

   ● are currently on bail.

3   However, if a disqualified person serves as a juror it does not necessarily make the verdict unsafe (*R v Richardson* (2004)).

4   Some categories of people used to be ineligible to serve on a jury. These included the Judiciary and others who have been concerned in the administration of justice within the last ten years.

5   Some people used to have the right to be excused from jury service. These included:

- those over the age of 65;
- Members of Parliament;
- members of the medical professions;
- members of the forces.

6   Jury ineligibility has been abolished by the Criminal Justice Act 2003. Judges and others in the administration of justice are now eligible for jury service.

7   In *R v Abdroikov* (2007), the House of Lords considered three cases in which police or others working in the administration of justice had sat as jurors. The Lords decided that the most important principle was that 'justice had to be seen to be done'. They held:

- the fact that a police officer was on the jury did not make a trial automatically unfair;
- however, where the officer on the jury worked from the same police station as police giving evidence against the defendant, then this meant that justice was not being seen to be done;
- allowing a senior Crown Prosecutor for the area to sit on a jury also meant that justice was not being seen to be done.

8   In *Hanif v UK* (2012), the European Court of Human Rights ruled that it was a breach of Art 6 (the right to a fair trial) where one of the jury was a serving police officer who knew one of the prosecution witnesses.

9   Mentally disordered persons are exempt from service.

10   Excusal as of right has been abolished by the Criminal Justice Act 2003. MPs, doctors and other medical staff will no longer be able to refuse to do jury service, though they can ask for a discretionary excusal.

11   Once summonsed for jury service it is possible to apply for discretionary excusal. This will only be granted if there is good reason, such as being too ill to attend. Jury service can also be deferred where the date given is inconvenient, eg because of examinations or business commitments.

15.2.3 Selection of a jury panel

1   Names are selected at random from the electoral register for the area in which the court is situated. The selection is done by computer at the Central Summoning Bureau.

2   Those names chosen may be vetted for criminal convictions via the police computer data of criminal records (*R v Sheffield Crown Court, ex p Brownlow* (1980), *R v Mason* (1980)).

3   In exceptional cases, a juror's background and political affiliation may be vetted. This should only occur in cases involving national security or terrorism. The Attorney-General must give permission for vetting (*Practice Note (Jury: Stand by: Jury Checks)* (1988)).

4   At court both prosecution and defence can challenge individual jurors for cause (s 12 Juries Act 1974).

5   There may also be a challenge to the array, ie the whole jury panel, on the basis that it was chosen in an unrepresentative and biased way (s 5 Juries Act 1974).

6   However, the fact that a jury does not contain any ethnic minority jurors is not a ground for challenge (*R v Ford* (1989)).

7   The prosecution may stand by individual jurors without giving a reason, but this right should be used sparingly (*Practice Note (Jury: Stand by: Jury Checks)* (1988)).

8   The judge may discharge any juror whom he thinks lacks the capacity to act effectively as a juror (s 9 Juries Act 1974).

15.2.4 Problems with selection

1   Not all people, especially the young and ethnic minorities, are registered to vote. The use of the electoral register excludes these. It also excludes homeless people.

2   Although the selection is random, this may not produce a cross-section of society.

3   There are too many discretionary excusals – Ministry of Justice research found that in 2005 only 64 per cent of those summoned served as jurors. This further undermines the representativeness of the jury.

4   Vetting is considered an invasion of privacy, but the Court of Appeal has ruled that it is lawful (*R v Mason* (1980), *R v McCann* (1990)).

15.2.5 The role of the jury in criminal cases

1   A jury is used in less than 2% of criminal cases.

2   There is a split function between the judge and the jury. The jury decides the facts and the judge decides the law.

3   The jury decides the verdict of guilty or not guilty. If the defendant is found guilty, the judge decides the sentence.

4   The judge cannot place pressure on the jury (*Bushell's* case (1670), *R v McKenna* (1960)).

5   The jury's verdict can be unanimous or, after at least two hours' deliberation, by a majority of 10 to 2 or 11 to 1.

6   Where the verdict is by majority, s 17(3) Juries Act 1974 states that the foreman of the jury must state in court the number agreeing and the number disagreeing with the verdict. However, the Court of Appeal has held that, provided the number agreeing with verdict is within the allowed majority, there is no need for the foreman to state also how many disagreed (*R v Pigg* (1983)).

15.2.6 Advantages of juries

1   There is public involvement in the legal system which makes the system more open.

2   The defendant is tried by his peers.

3   There is public confidence in the use of juries.

4   They are 'the lamp that shows that freedom lives' (Lord Devlin).

5   The use of 12 jurors should cancel out any individual bias.

6   The jury is independent. This allows the members to come to a 'just' verdict as opposed to a 'legal' verdict (*Ponting's* case (1985), *R v Randle and Pottle* (1991)).

15.2.7 Disadvantages of juries

1   The jury's decision is reached in secret. The reasons for that decision are not known. Evidence of what occurred in the jury room is not normally allowed (*R v Thompson* (1962)).

2   In some cases the jury has used unreliable means of coming to a decision, eg in *R v Young* (1995), where a ouija board was used to contact the dead victims.

3   Jurors may be racially biased, as in *Sander v United Kingdom* (2000), where the European Court of Human Rights ruled that a jury should have been discharged.

4   The House of Lords has ruled that discussions in the jury room must remain secret and disclosure, even where it showed a problem, could not

be allowed to affect a verdict once the verdict had been given (*R v Connor; R v Mirza* (2004)).

5   Jurors may not be able to understand complicated cases. There is provision in the Criminal Justice Act 2003 for complex fraud cases to be tried by a judge alone but this provision will only become law if both Houses of Parliament approve any regulations made for it.

6   Media coverage may influence a jury's verdict, especially in high- profile cases.

7   Jurors are increasingly likely to research cases on the internet (*R v Karakaya* (2005)).

8   The compulsory nature of jury service is unpopular.

9   Jurors can be 'nobbled'. In *R v Twomey* (2009), the Court of Appeal (under powers in s 44 of the Criminal Justice Act 2003) made the first order that a trial should be held by a judge alone, after earlier trials had collapsed because of attempts to 'nobble' the jury.

10   Acquittal rates in the Crown Court are criticised for being too high. However, a large number of acquittals are directed by the judge. The jury acquits in about 36% of cases.

11   The use of a jury makes a case longer and more expensive.

15.2.8 Special problems of civil juries

1   In civil cases the jury decides the issue of liability and also the amount of damages to be paid.

2   Civil juries may be biased against newspapers or well-known personalities involved in libel cases.

3   The amount of damages is unpredictable and inconsistent. However, on appeal the Court of Appeal can substitute the amount it feels is proper (s 8 Courts and Legal Services Act 1990).

4   Juries add very heavily to the costs of the case. The losing party is likely to face a bill of hundreds of thousands of pounds.

Key Cases Checklist

Use of juries in civil cases

Ward v James (1966)
A jury should not normally be used in personal injury cases

H v Ministry of Defence (1991)
Exceptional circumstances are not sufficient in personal injury cases to justify trial by jury

Racz v Home Office (1994)
A close relationship to one of the torts where jury trial is normally ordered is not a factor to be taken into consideration

Goldsmith v Pressdram Ltd (1987)
Even where reputation is at stake, jury trial can be refused if the documentation is complicated

Use of juries in criminal cases

R v Twomey and others (2009)
Order made for trial by a judge alone after jury tampering

KS v R (2010)
Order made for trial by a judge alone refused as there were ways of avoiding jury tampering

Juries use and qualifications

Qualifications of jurors

R v Richardson (2004)
The fact that a juror was disqualified because of a criminal conviction did not make a verdict unsafe

R v Abdroikov (2005)
An eligible juror should not be excluded merely because of their knowledge of the criminal justice system

Hanif v UK (2012)
Where a juror knows a witness it is a breach of the right to fair trial

---

15.1   *R v Twomey and others* [2009] EWCA Crim 1035

Key Facts

Ds were charged in connection with offences connected to a major robbery from a warehouse at Heathrow airport. Three previous trials had collapsed and there had been a serious attempt at jury tampering in the last of these. The prosecution applied, under the provisions of s 44 of the Criminal Justice Act 2003, for trial by a judge alone. The Court of Appeal ordered that the trial should be by judge alone.

Key Law

Trial should be by judge alone as there was a very signifi-cant risk of jury tampering. Protective measures could not sufficiently address the extent of the risk. Also the proposed protective measures would have imposed a real burden on individual jurors.

15.1   *KS v R* [2010] EWCA Crim 1756   CA

Key Facts

An associate of D had tried to tamper with the jury during D's trial at Northampton Crown Court. As a result, the jury had to be discharged. The prosecution applied for the re-trial to take place without a jury under s 44 of the Criminal Justice Act 2003. A single judge granted this, but the Court of Appeal overturned the decision.

Key Law

The attempt to tamper with the jury had been opportunistic. It arose because of the 'casual arrangements' at the court for smokers, which enabled members of the public to mix with jurors. There was no evidence of careful planning. A fairly limited level of jury protection could reasonably be provided and this would outweigh the potential threat of future jury tampering in the case.

15.1   *Ward v James* [1966] 1 All ER 563   CA

Key Facts

The claimant (C) was a passenger in a car which was involved in an accident. C was paralysed as a result and started an action in negligence against the car driver. C applied for trial by jury: this was ordered, but the Court of Appeal made *obiter* statements that the use of juries in personal injury cases should not be encouraged.

Key Law

A jury should not normally be used in a personal injury trial.

Key Judgment: Lord Denning MR

'Recent cases show the desirability of three things. First, assessability: in cases of grave injury, where the body is wrecked or the brain destroyed, it is very difficult to assess a fair compensation in money, so difficult that the award must basically be a conventional figure, derived from experience or from awards in comparable cases. Secondly, uniformity: there should be some measure of *uniformity* in awards so that similar decisions are given in similar cases; otherwise there will be great dissatisfaction in the community, and much criticism of the administration of justice. Thirdly, *predictability*: parties should be able to predict with some measure of accuracy the sum which is likely to be awarded in a particular case . . . None of these three is achieved when the damages are left at large to the jury.'

15.1

Hodges v Harland & Wolff [1965] 1 All ER 1086

CA

Key Facts

The claimant was operating an air compressor in the course of his work. The spindle on the machine was not properly guarded and it caught the claimant's trousers and tore away his penis and scrotum. He was left with the urge for sexual activity but was unable to perform the sexual act. He applied for the case to be tried with a jury and the Court of Appeal granted this.

Key Law

Trial by jury in personal injury cases should only be allowed in exceptional cases.

Key Comment

In this case the Court of Appeal stated that the comments made in *Ward v James* did not mean that personal injuries cases could never be tried by a jury. However, this case appears to have been the last personal injury case to have been tried by jury.

15.1

H v Ministry of Defence [1991] 2 All ER 834

Key Facts

A soldier received negligent medical treatment which led to the need for a major part of his penis to be amputated. He applied for trial by jury but this was refused.

Key Law

The policy should be that as stated in *Ward v James*, ie that trial by jury is inappropriate for any personal injury action so far as the jury is required to assess compensating damages.

15.1

Racz v Home Office [1994] 2 WLR 23

Key Facts

The claimant alleged that he had been held in prison on remand without justification. He made a claim for damages for misfeasance in public office in respect of the period for which he had been detained. He sought jury trial for this claim. Trial by jury was refused despite the fact that the action was closely related to false imprisonment. The fact that the claimant sought exemplary damages was also insufficient to justify trial by jury

Key Law

Section 69(3) of the Supreme Court Act 1981 raises a presumption against jury trial. The fact that a claim has a close relationship to one of the torts for which s 69(1) retained the right to jury trial was not a factor to be taken into account in deciding whether it is appropriate to rebut the presumption.

Key Comment

This decision illustrates the reluctant of the courts to order trial by jury in civil actions.

15.1   *Goldsmith v Pressdram Ltd* [1987] 3 All ER 485   CA

Key Facts

The claimant (C) was a director of a number of large inter-national companies. The defendants (Ds) published an article in the satirical magazine, Private Eye, alleging that the claimant had been involved in secret share dealings. C started a defamation action against Ds. Ds applied for the case to be tried by a judge alone on the basis that their defence would involve detailed examination of complex multiple transactions carried out by the claimant. The judge made this order and the Court of Appeal upheld it.

Key Law

In deciding whether a case should be tried by jury, the fact that the alleged defamation concerned criminal conduct was not enough to outweigh the problems of lengthy exam-ination of documents.

Key Judgment: Lawton LJ

'It is true that the allegation against [the claimant] is an unpleasant one. It charges him with criminal offences. His reputation, honour and integrity are, to some extent, in issue, but . . . the fact that honour and integrity are under attack in a case is not an overriding factor in favour of trial with a jury . . . This case, although it may be of importance to [the claimant], cannot be said to be one affecting national interest or national personalities. It is a long way from such a case and, having regard to its undoubted complexity and the difficulties which a jury will have in following the detail of evidence, in my judgment the discretion of the court should not be exercised in favour of the [claimant].'

15.2   *R v Richardson* [2004] EWCA Crim 2997   CA

Key Facts

A person with a criminal conviction which disqualified them from sitting as a juror, sat as a juror. D appealed against his conviction on the basis that the presence of a disqualified person on the jury made the verdict unsafe.

Key Law

The fact that a juror was disqualified because of a criminal conviction did not make a verdict unsafe.

Key Judgment

The court cited with approval the judgment of Garland J in *R v Bliss* (1986) where he said that the Court of Appeal 'will not interfere with the verdict of a jury unless there is either evidence pointing directly to the fact or evidence from which a proper inference may be drawn that the defendant may have been prejudiced or may not have received a fair trial.'

15.2   *R v Abdroikov* [2005] EWCA Crim 1986

Key Facts

Three cases were heard together on appeal. In two of the cases a police officer had been on the jury; in the third case a CPS lawyer was on the jury. The defendants appealed on the basis that this made the trials appear unfair. The appeals were dismissed.

Key Law

Where a person was eligible to sit as a juror, they should not be excluded merely because of their knowledge of the criminal justice system.

Key Judgment: Lord Woolf CJ

'A fair-minded and informed observer would not conclude that there was a real possibility that a juror was biased merely because his occupation was one which meant that he was involved in some capacity or other in the administration of justice.'

Key Comment

Prior to April 2004, people who were involved in the administration of justice (or who had been within the previous 10 years) were ineligible to sit as jurors. This ineligibility was removed by the Criminal Justice Act 2003.

15.2

Hanif v United Kingdom 52999/08 (2012) 55 EHRR 16, [2012] Crim LR 295

ECH

Key Facts

A police officer was selected as a juror. He immediately alerted the court to the fact that he knew one of the prosecution police witnesses. It was particularly important as the evidence of this witness was crucial to the case against the defendant. However, the trial judge had ruled that this did not matter. The case continued with the police officer juror being the foreman of the jury and the defendant was convicted.

Key Law

The European Court of Human Rights ruled that having a police officer on the jury in these circumstances was a breach of Article 6(1) of the European Convention on Human Rights – the right to a fair trial.

Jury selection

R v Sheffield Crown Court, ex p Brownlow (1980)
Jury vetting is a breach of privacy and unconstitutional

R v Mason (1980)
The court can inquire into happenings outside the jury room

R v Ford (1989)
If a jury has been randomly selected it cannot be challenged even if it contains no ethnic minority jurors

Bushells' case (1670)
The jury is the sole arbiter of fact and must not be pressurised by the judge

R v McKenna (1960)
The jury must not be put under undue pressure when coming to a verdict

R v Pigg (1983)
It is sufficient if the foreman announces the number of jurors who agreed with verdict on a finding by a majority verdict

---

Juries – selection and secrecy of the jury room

Secrecy of the jury room

R v Thompson (1962)
Evidence of what occurred in the jury room is not admissible

R v Young (1995)
The court can inquire into happenings outside the jury room

R v Connor: R v Mirza (2004)
The rule that the court cannot hear evidence of events in the jury room is compatible with Art 6 (right to fair trial) of the European Convention on Human Rights

R v Karakaya (2005)
Jurors must decide the case on the evidence given in court. They cannot take into account outside information

---

15.2.3

R v Sheffield Crown Court, ex p Brownlow [1980] 2 All ER 444

Key Facts

Two police officers were due to be tried at the Crown Court on charges of assault. The defence solicitors sought an order that the prospective jury members be checked for criminal convictions.

The judge made an order that the Chief Constable carry out such a check. The Chief Constable applied to the Divisional Court for the judge's order to be quashed. This was refused on the procedural point that the Divisional Court had no jurisdiction to review decisions made by a Crown Court judge. This point went to the Court of Appeal who confirmed that the Divisional Court had no jurisdiction. In the course of their judgments *obiter* comments were made on jury vetting.

Key Law

Obiter statement that jury vetting is a breach of privacy and is unconstitutional.

Key Judgment: Lord Denning MR

'To my mind it is unconstitutional for the police authorities to engage in "jury vetting". So long as a person is eligible of jury service and is not disqualified, I cannot think it right that, behind his back, the police should go through his record . . . If this sort of thing is to be allowed, what comes of a man's right to privacy?'

 15.2.3 *R v Mason* [1980] 3 All ER 777

Key Facts

D was tried for burglary and handling stolen property. Before the trial began, the police had checked the names of those summoned for jury service and given details of convictions to the prosecution. These convictions did not disqualify any juror from serving, but the prosecution used the information to ask for a panel member to stand by for the Crown (i.e. not be used as a juror unless there were insufficient others to form a panel). D argued on appeal that this was in breach of guidelines on jury vetting issued by the Attorney-General.

Key Law

Some scrutiny of the jury panel is necessary to ensure that disqualified persons are prevented from sitting on a jury. If such checks reveal other non-disqualifying convictions, then it is lawful for these to be given to the prosecution.

15.2.3   *R v Ford* **[1989] 3 All ER 445**   CA

Key Facts

The defendant, who was charged with driving without consent and reckless driving, was from an ethnic minority. The jury panel was entirely white. D applied for a multi-racial jury. The application was refused.

Key Law

Random selection is the basis of jury selection. A jury that has been correctly randomly selected cannot be changed just because it does not contain any ethnic minority members.

Key Judgment: Lord Lane LCJ

'The conclusion is that, however well intentioned the judge's motive might be, the judge has no power to influence the composition of the jury, and that it is wrong for him to attempt to do so. If it should ever become desirable that the principle of random selection should be altered, that will have to be done by way of statute and cannot be done by any judicial decision.'

15.2.5   *Bushell's Case* **(1670) Vaugh 135**

Key Facts

Several jurors refused to convict Quaker activists of unlawful assembly. The trial judge would not accept the not guilty verdict, and ordered the jurors to resume their deliberations without food or drink. When the jurors persisted in their refusal to convict, they were fined and committed to prison until the fines were paid. On appeal, the Court of Common Pleas ordered the release of the jurors, holding that jurors could not be punished for their verdict.

Key Law

A judge cannot pressurise a jury to return the verdict which he thinks is appropriate. The jury is the sole arbiter of fact in a criminal trial.

15.2.5 *R v McKenna* [1960] 1 QB 411 CCA

Key Facts

The judge at the trial threatened the jury, who had been deliberating for about 2 hours and 15 minutes, that if they did not return a verdict within another 10 minutes they would be locked up all night. The jury then returned a verdict of guilty within six minutes. The defendant's conviction was quashed on appeal because of the judge putting undue pressure on the jury.

Key Law

The jury, when coming to their verdict, must not be subject to undue pressure by the judge.

Key Judgment: Cassels J

'It is a cardinal principle of our criminal law that in considering their verdict, concerning as it does, the liberty of the subject, a jury shall deliberate in complete freedom, uninfluenced by any promise, unintimidated by any threat. They still stand between the Crown and the subject, and they are still one of the main defences of personal liberty. To say to such a tribunal in the course of its deliberations that it must reach a conclusion within ten minutes or else undergo hours of personal inconvenience and discomfort, is a disservice to the cause of justice.'

15.2.5 *R v Pigg* [1983] 1 All ER 56 HL

Key Facts

When the foreman of the jury returned the jury's decision, he stated that it was a majority verdict and that 10 of the jury had agreed with the verdict. He did not state how many jurors had disagreed.

Key Law

Provided the foreman announced the number who had agreed with the verdict and that number was within the number allowed for a majority verdict, then the conviction was legal. It did not matter that the foreman had not also been asked how many disagreed with the verdict.

15.2.7   ***R v Thompson* [1962] 1 All ER 65**   CCA

Key Facts

After the jury had announced a verdict of guilty but before the judge had passed sentence, one of the jurors told a member of the public that the jury had been in favour of acquitting D until the foreman had produced a list of the defendant's previous convictions. D appealed against his conviction but the Court of Criminal Appeal refused to accept evidence of what happened in the jury room and upheld the conviction.

Key Law

It is important to preserve the secrecy of the jury room. Evidence of what occurred in jury discussions cannot be given in evidence to support an appeal.

15.2.7   ***R v Young* [1995] QB 324**   CA

Key Facts

The defendant was charged with the murder of two people. The jury had to stay overnight in a hotel as they had not reached a verdict by the end of the first day of discussion. During this stay at the hotel, four members of the jury held a seance using a ouija board to try to contact the dead victims and ask who had killed them. The next day the jury returned a verdict of guilty. When the fact that the ouija board had been used became known, the defendant appealed and the Court of Appeal quashed the verdict and ordered a re-trial of the case.

Key Law

The court can inquire into what happened where the incident was not part of the jury discussions in the jury room.

15.2.7   ### *Sander v United Kingdom* [2000] Crim LR 767   ECJ

Key Facts

During the trial one juror wrote a note to the judge raising concern over the fact that other jurors had been openly making racist remarks and jokes. The judge asked the jury to 'search their consciences'. The next day the judge received two letters, one signed by all the jurors (including the juror who had made the complaint) in which they denied any racist attitudes and a second from one juror who admitted that he may have been the one making racist jokes. Despite the discrepancy between the two letters, the judge allowed the case to continue. The ECHR held that in these circumstances the judge should have discharged the jury as there was an obvious risk of racial bias.

Key Law

Where the judge is alerted to an obvious risk of racial bias before the trial ends then he has power to discharge the jury.

15.2.7   ### *R v Connor: R v Mirza (conjoined appeals)* [2004] UKHL 4   HL

R v Connor

Key Facts

The two defendants were jointly charged with wounding. They were both convicted by a majority verdict of 10–2. Five days after the verdict (but before sentence was passed) one of the jurors wrote to the Crown Court stating that while many jurors thought it was one or other of the defendants who had committed the stabbing, they would convict both to 'teach them a lesson'. The complaining juror said that,

when she argued that the jury should consider which defendant was responsible, her co-jurors had refused to listen and remarked that if they did that they could be a week considering verdicts in the case.
R v Mirza

Key Facts

The defendant was a Pakistani who settled in the UK in 1988. He had an interpreter to help him in the trial and during the trial the jury sent notes asking why he needed an interpreter. He was convicted on a 10–2 majority. Six days after the jury verdict, one juror wrote to the defendant's counsel alleging that from the start of the trial there had been a 'theory' that the use of an interpreter was a 'ploy'. The juror also said that she had been shouted down when she objected and reminded her fellow jurors of the judge's directions.

Key Law

The common law rule which protected jurors' confidentiality and which precluded the court from admitting evidence of what had happened in the jury room after the verdict had been given is still effective. This rule is compatible with Art 6 of the European Convention on Human Rights.

15.2.7 ### *R v Karakaya* [2005] EWCA Crim 346   CA

Key Facts

A juror did an Internet search and brought the information into the jury room during deliberations following an overnight adjournment. The print outs were discovered by the jury bailiff. D's conviction was quashed as being unsafe.

Key Law

This contravened the fundamental rule that no evidence was to be introduced after the jury had retired to consider their verdict.

Key Link

R v Gearing [1968] 1 WLR 344.

16 Legal services and funding

```
                    ┌─────────────────────────┐
                    │     HELP FOR FUNDING     │
                    └─────────────────────────┘
```

CIVIL CASES

Advice
- Lawyers or advice agencies

Representation
- Only certain types of cases qualify
- Must show case should be funded
- Must qualify financially

Private help
- Conditional fee agreements
- Some *pro bono* representation available

CRIMINAL CASES

Advice
- Duty solicitor at police station
- Duty solicitor at Magistrates' Court

Representation
- Available if in the interests of justice
- Must qualify financial

Private help
- Must pay full fee
- Conditional fee agreements NOT allowed

▶ 16.1 Public funding for civil cases

1   The organisation of public funding of civil cases was changed by the Legal Aid, Sentencing and Punishment of Offenders Act 2012.

2   The previous system, which had been completely independent of the Government, was criticised for its financial management.

3   Public funding is now managed by the Legal Aid Agency which is under the umbrella of the Ministry of Justice. Its head is the Director of Casework, an independent civil servant.

16.1.1 Legal Aid for civil cases

1   Legal aid is only available for the categories of civil cases mentioned in the Legal Aid, Sentencing and Punishment of Offenders Act 2012 or regulations made under the Act.

2   It is no longer available for medical negligence cases, trespass to the person, land or property. All these types of case were previously eligible for legal aid.

3   Cases now eligible are mainly those involving liberty of the person or issues that affect children.

16.1.2 Funding criteria

1   The person must show that their case should be funded. To decide this, the following points are considered:

- the likely cost of funding and the benefit which may be obtained;
- the availability of resources to provide services;
- the importance of the matters for the individual;
- the availability of other services such as mediation;
- where the services sought are in relation to a dispute, the prospects of success in the dispute;
- the public interest.

2   The person must qualify financially. To decide this, their disposable income and disposable capital are calculated.

3   Disposable income is the amount of income available to a person after taking into account essential living expenses.

4   Disposable capital is the assets owned by the person. It includes the equitable value of the home above £100,000.

5   If disposable income and capital are below the minimum limits, the person will receive free funding. If their disposable income and capital are above the maximum allowed, then they do not qualify for help. If their disposable income and capital are between the minimum and maximum figures, they will have to pay a contribution towards the cost of the funding.

6   The limits are quite low, eg anyone with more than £8,000 capital will not qualify.

16.1.3 Problems with funding of civil cases

1   Only about 1,700 firms of solicitors have contracts. This is less than a third of the number who previously did legal aid work. There are problems of access to justice in some areas where there is no solicitor doing publicly funded work.

2   Even solicitors who do publicly funded work are cutting back on the number of cases they take because of the low rates of pay.

3   As far back as 2004, the Citizens Advice Bureau reported that there were 'advice deserts' in some parts of the country where there were no legal aid solicitors available for important cases such as those involving housing or health law.

4   Only people on very low levels of income qualify for help.

5   The statutory charge (clawback of costs from damages) can mean that a claimant has very little left from their damages even though they won the case.

▶ 16.2 Private funding for civil cases

Paying privately for a lawyer is very expensive, especially in London. Most individuals who do not qualify for help and representation under the government scheme cannot afford to pay full private fees. For this reason conditional fee agreements have been developed.

16.2.1 Conditional fees

1   These were first allowed by the Courts and Legal Services Act 1990 and extended by the Access to Justice Act 1999.

2   The solicitor and client agree on the fee that would normally be charged for such a case, with a 'success fee' payable if the case is won.

3   If the solicitor does not win the case, then the client pays nothing. If the solicitor is successful, then the client pays the normal fee plus the success fee.

4   The Legal Aid, Sentencing and Punishment of Offenders Act 2012 (LASPO) states that the amount of the success fee cannot be claimed as part of the costs of the case by a winning party. Previously it could be claimed.

5   It is possible to insure against losing a case. However, if the case is won, LASPO does not allow the court to order the losing party to pay the cost of insurance premiums. Previously it could be claimed.

6   These two changes mean that a winning party will have to pay the success fee and insurance themselves, thus making the use of conditional fees less financially attractive.

❱ 16.3 Advice agencies

Free advice can be obtained from a number of agencies. Some of them specialise in a particular area of law, while others give general advice. Some examples are:

- the Citizens Advice Bureau;
- law centres;
- Community Legal Advice Centres;
- the Bar's Free Representation Unit which represents litigants in court.

❱ 16.4 Legal aid in criminal cases

1   Legal aid for criminal cases is also the responsibility of the Director of Casework and the Legal Aid Agency.

2   This service is aimed at 'securing that individuals involved in criminal investigations or proceedings have access to such advice, assistance and representation as the interests of justice require'.

16.4.1 Advice and assistance

1   There is a duty solicitor scheme for people who are arrested and held in custody at a police station. This is free.

2   When someone is arrested, the custody officer at the police station must tell them about this scheme.

3   Advice is usually given by telephone, but if a suspect is being interviewed by the police they may have a solicitor present at the interview.

4   There is also a duty solicitor scheme at many Magistrates' Courts for people to receive free advice on their cases. The solicitor may also represent them on matters such as bail applications.

16.4.2 Representation

1   A defendant should have a legal representative paid for by the State where it is 'in the interests of justice'.

2   In deciding this, five categories are considered. These are whether:

- the individual would, if any matter arising in the proceedings is decided against him, be likely to lose his liberty or livelihood or suffer serious damage to his reputation;

- the case will involve consideration of a point of law;
- the individual is unable to understand the proceedings or to state his own case;
- the case may involve the tracing, interviewing or expert cross-examination of witnesses;
- it is in the interests of another person that the individual should be represented.

3   There is a strict means test for defendants in the Magistrates' Courts. They will only qualify for publicly funded representation if they are on a low level of income.

4   All defendants in the Crown Court can receive legal aid, but the higher their income the higher the contribution they will have to pay. Also, where a defendant is found guilty, they may have to pay a further amount from their capital.

Index

absolute discharge 142
activist and passive judges 18–19,
        55
Acts of Parliament 36
    advantages over case law 40
    amendment or repeal 44
    coming into force 40
    drafting process 37–8
    Green and White Papers 37
    Parliamentary Act (1911 and
            1949) powers 39–40
    Parliamentary sovereignty 40–1
    pre-parliamentary process and
            consultation 37
    resulting from Law Commission
            reports 85–6
    statute law 3
    see also Bills
Administrative Justice and
        Tribunals Council
        (AJTC) 105–6, 107
administrative tribunals 103
advocacy, negligent 150, 151,
        152–3
advocacy rights/rights of audience
        147, 148, 149
Advocates-General 73, 74
alcohol treament requirement 142
alternative business structures
        (ABSs) 150–1
alternative dispute resolution
        (ADR) 94–5
    cases 96, 99–102
    encouraging 91, 93

amendments
    Acts of Parliament 44
    delegated legislation 42
anti-social behaviour order 143
appeals
    civil cases 91–3
    see also Court of Appeal; *specific
            courts*
appropriate adult 116
arbitration 94–5
arrest
    other powers 114
    police powers of 112–13, 119,
            121–3
    procedure 114
    warrants 114, 130
Attorney-General 133
Austin, J. 1

bail 127–8
    balancing conflicting interests
            128–9
    failure to attend police station
            114
    Magistrates' Court decision
            130
    special cases 128
Bar Council 149–50
Bar Professional Training Course
        (BPTC) 148
barristers 147–8
    Bar Council 149–50
    Queen's Council (QC) 148
    role 148

suing (negligent advocacy) 150,
        151, 152–3
    training 147–8
bias
    judiciary 159
    juries 174, 175
Bills 37, 38
    introducing to Parliament 38
    law reform 85
    passing 39
    types of 39
binding precedent 9, 19, 20–2
Bland case 5–6
breach of civil rights 118
breach of natural justice 106
by-laws 41, 42

case law *see* common law/case law
case management
    civil 97–8
    criminal 135
caution 116
Chancery courts/Division 4, 88, 156
child safety order 143
Circuit Judges 92, 156
Citizen's Advise Bureau 192, 193
civil justice system 87
    allocation of cases 90
        three tracks 88, 90–1
    appeal routes and approaches
        91–3
    court structure 88–9
    funding 190–3
    juries 171, 175, 176, 177–81
    lay magistrates 166
    Magistrates' Court 130
    post-Woolf reforms 93
    procedure (CPR 1999) 89, 91,
        96–8
    proceedings against police 118
    timetables 96, 98
    see also alternative dispute
        resolution (ADR)

civil law
    and common law, distinctions
        between 4
    and criminal law, distinctions
        between 4–5
Civil Procedure Rules 1999 89, 91,
        96–8
civil rights, breach of 118
classification of law 2–4
    by source 3–4
    by type 3
clerks, Magistrates' 166, 167, 168–9
commissions/committees, temporary
        86
Committee of the Regions 73
common law/case law 4
    Acts of Parliament, advantages
        over 40
    different meanings of 4
community orders 140, 141–2, 143
compensation orders 140
complaints against police 118
conciliation 94
conditional discharge 142
conditional fees 192
confession 116
consent
    to enter and search premises 112
    to fingerprinting and samples
        117
Constitutional Reform Act 2005
        158, 160
consultation
    Acts of Parliament 37
    delegated legislation 42
contempt of court 5
conveyancers, licenced 149
Council of the European Union 72
County Court 11, 88, 89, 92
    Circuit Judges 156
    District Judges 155
    legal executives 149
    recorders 156

Court of Appeal 11
    Civil Division 14, 15–16
    Criminal Division 14, 16, 33–4,
        132–3
    and judicial precedent 14–16,
        26–33
    jury verdicts 174
    law reporting 10
    Lord Justices of Appeal 156
    multi-track civil cases 92
    tribunals 104
court hierarchy 10–11, 19, 21–3
Court Rules Committees 41
court rulings, outside English legal
        system 9
CPS *see* Crown Prosecution
        Service (CPS)
Criminal Case Review Commission
        (CCRC) 134
criminal courts 126
    see also specific courts
criminal law
    and civil law, distinctions
        between 4–5
    classification of offences 129–34
Criminal Law Revision
        Committee 86
Criminal Procedure Rules 134–5
criminal proceedings
    against police 118–19
    juries 173–4, 176–7
    lay magistrates 166
    Legal Aid, advice and
        representation 193–4
    miscarriages of justice 134
Crown Court 11, 132
    acquittals 175
    appeals from 132–4
    appeals from Magistrates'
        Court 131, 132
    Circuit Judges 156
    classification of offences 129
    CPS representation 127

fines 142
juries 171
legal aid 193
miscarriages of justice 134
recorders 156
Crown Prosecution Service (CPS)
    127
    barristers employed by 147–8
    solicitors employed by 147
curfew, as condition of bail 128
custodial sentences 139, 140–1
custody officer's role 115, 116, 193
'custody plus' 141

defendant, appeals by 132–3
delegated legislation 41
    cases 44, 46–7
    control of 42–3
    disadvantages of 43–4
    need for 41–2
    regulatory law 4
    types of 41
Denning, Lord 15, 55, 58
denunciation, sentencing as 140
Deputy District Judges 155–6
'deservedness versus dangerousness'
    139
detention at police station 115–18
    cases 119, 122–5
    custody officer's role 115, 116,
        193
    interviews 116
    right to legal advice 115–16, 193
    searches, samples and
        fingerprinting 117–18
    time limits 115
deterrence, sentencing as 138
Dilhorne, Viscount 55
Director of Public Prosecutions 127
distinguishing 17, 32, 33–4
District Judges 91–2, 155–6
divisional courts 11
domestic tribunals 106–7

double liability 5
drug rehabilitation requirement 142
duty solicitor scheme 193

Economic and Social Committee
          (EU) 73
ejusdem generis 53
electronic tagging 128, 139
employment tribunals 104
enabling Act 42, 43
equity law 4
European approach to statutory
          interpretation 49, 54
European Commission 72
European Convention on Human
          Rights 38, 41, 54–5,
          92, 128
European Court of Human
          Rights 10
    and Court of Appeal 14, 15
    juries 172, 174
European Court of Justice 10, 54,
          73–4
European Directives 53, 54, 75–6
European Parliament 73
European Union law 71–2
    institutions 72–4
    and Parliamentary sovereignty
          76–7
    sources of law 74–6, 78, 79–81
    supremacy of 41, 78, 80–2
excluded evidence 116, 119, 124–5
expert witnesses 90, 91
expressio unius est exclusio alterius 53
extrinsic aids to statutory
          interpretation 52–3, 56,
          64–8

Family Division 88
fast track cases 88, 90
    appeals 91–2
fines 130, 142
fingerprinting 117

general deterrence 138
Golden Rule 50, 52, 59–61
Government Bills 37, 38
government policy 37
Graduate Diploma in Law
          146, 147
Green Papers 37
guilty plea 144

Hansard 53, 55
Hansard Society: *Making the Law*
          Report 37
Hart, H.L.A. 2, 136–7
'Henry VIII' clauses 44
hierarchy of courts 10–11, 19,
          22–3
High Court 11, 88, 92, 133
High Court Judges 92, 156
Home Secretary 107
hospital orders 143
House of Commons 38, 39, 40
House of Lords 10, 11
    Bills 38, 39, 40, 42
    Delegated Powers Scrutiny
          Committee 42
    Judicial Committee,
          replacement of 158
    and judicial precedent *see*
          Practice Statement
    jury discussions 174–5
    see also Supreme Court
Human Rights Act 1998
    statutory interpretation 54–5
    tribunals 106
Hybrid Bill 39

imprisonment 139, 140–1
incapacitation methods 138–9
independence of judiciary 158–9,
          160–2
Independent Police Complaints
          Commission (IPCC) 118
indictable offences 129, 130

individual deterrence 138
inferior courts *see* County
        Court; Crown Court;
        Magistrates' Court
inferior judges 155–6, 158
Inns of Court 148
inquiries 107–8
Institute of Legal Executives (ILEX)
        146, 149, 156
international Conventions 52
international and national law 3
    conflict between 76–7
Internet: law reporting 10
interviews, at police station
        115–16
intimate samples 117
intimate searches 117

Joint Select Committee on
        Statutory Instruments
        42–3
Judicial Appointments Commission
        104, 155
Judicial Committee of the Privy
        Council *see* Privy Council
judicial law-making 18–19, 34–5
    common law/case law 4
judicial precedent *see* precedent
judicial review 106, 107
Judicial Studies Board (JSB) 157
judiciary 154
    activist and passive 18–19, 55
    appointment 155–7
    bias 159
    immunity from suit 159
    independence 158–9, 160–2
    law reform 86
    removal 157–8
    statutory interpretation by 55
    training 157
juries 170
    advantages and disadvantages
        of 174–5

civil cases 171, 175, 176, 177–82
criminal cases 173–4, 176–7
discretionary excusals 172, 173
exemptions/ineligibility 171–2
'nobbled' 171, 175
qualifications and
        disqualifications 171,
        176, 180–2
secrecy of jury room 174–5, 183,
        187–9
selection and selection problems
        172–3, 182–6
use of 171
vetting 173
Justices of the Supreme Court 156

language rules of statutory
        interpretation 53, 55,
        67–9
law, definition of 1
Law Commission 37, 52, 84–5
    achievements of 85–6
    composition and working 84
    implementation of reports 85
law reform 83
    bodies 86
    need for 84
    see also Law Commission
Law Reform Committee 86
law reporting 9–10
Law Society 146, 149, 150
lay magistrates 163
    advantages 166–7
    appointment 164
    cases 167, 168–9
    composition of Bench 164–5
    disadvantages 167
    Magistrates' clerk 166, 167,
        168–9
    qualifications 163–4
    retirement and removal 165–6
    role 166
    training 165

lay members of tribunals 104
legal advice
    agencies 193
    right to 115–16, 193
legal executives 149
legal funding 190
    civil cases 190–3
    criminal cases 193–4
Legal Practice Course (LPC) 146
legal profession 145
    cases 151–3
    para-legals 149
    regulation 149–51
    see also barristers; solicitors
Legal Services Act 2007 150–1
Legal Services Board 150
Legal Services Commission 147
Legal (Services) Ombudsman 149,
        150
legal system 2
Leggat Report 104
legislation see Acts of Parliament;
        delegated legislation;
        statutory interpretation
Legislative and Statutory
        Instrument Reform Act
        2006 43
licenced conveyancers 149
life imprisonment 139, 140, 141
Literal Rule 50, 52, 56–8
local advisory committees 164
local authority by-laws 41, 42, 43
Lord Chancellor 159–60
    equity law 4
    judicial appointments and
        independence 155,
        158
    and Law commission 84
    lay magistrates 164, 165–6
    Practice Statement 12
    QC appointments 148
Lord Chief Justice 158
Lord Justices of Appeal 156

Magistrates' Clerk 166, 167, 168–9
Magistrates' Court 11, 129–31
    appeals from 131
    CPS representation 127
    District Judges 155–6
    duty solicitor 193
    fines 142
    jurisdiction 129–30
    miscarriages of justice 134
    publicly funded resprensentation
        194
    sentencing 130
    Youth Court 130
mandatory order 106
media and juries 175
mediation 94
mental health treatment
        requirement 142
mentally ill offenders, sentencing
        of 143
minimum sentences 141
Minister of Justice 160
miscarriages of justice 134
Mischief Rule 50, 52, 60–3
'Money Bill' 39
morality and law 1–2
multi-track cases 88, 90–1
    appeals 92

natural justice rules 106
negligent advocacy 150, 153
negotiation 94
noscitur a sociis 53

obiter dicta 9, 17
Orders in Council 41
original precedence 8

para-legals 149
parent/guardian 130, 143
parenting order 143
Parliamentary Act (1911 and 1949)
        powers 39–40

Parliamentary Inquiries 107
Parliamentary sovereignty 40–1,
	44, 45
	and EU law 76–7
part-time judges 156, 157
passive and activist judges 18–19,
	54–5
per incuriam rule 15, 16, 26, 30–1
persuasive precedent 9
police
	complaints against 118
	inquiries 107, 108
	powers 109
		see also specific powers
Practice Statement 11–13, 18, 19,
	24–6
	and Court of Appeal 15
	need for 11–12
	use of 12–13
pre-sentence reports 144
precedent
	advantages and disadvantages
		17–18
	binding 9, 19, 20–2
	and Court of Appeal 14–16,
		26–33
	distinguishing 17, 32, 33–4
	hierarchy of courts 10–11, 19,
		21–2
	House of Lords *see* Practice
		Statement
	judicial law-making 18–19, 36–7
	law reporting 9–10
	obiter dicta 9, 17
	original 8
	persuasive 9
	and Privy Council 15, 32, 33
	ratio decidendi 9, 16, 17
	stare decisis 8
	Supreme Court 13
premises, police power to search
	111–12, 119, 121–2
'prerogative' orders 106

Private Bill 39
private funding in civil cases 192
private law 3
Private Member's Bill 38
Privy Council
	delegated legislation 41
	and judicial precedent 15, 32, 33
	and tribunals 106–7
Professional Diploma in Law 146,
	149
Professional Higher Diploma in Law
	146, 149
professional misconduct
	barristers 150
	solicitors 149
Professional Skills Course 146
prohibitory order 106
prosecution, appeals by 133
prosecutor-advocate 147
protection of society 138–9
Public Bill 39
public inquiries 107
public law 3
punishment 137–8
	definition of 136–7
pupillage 148
purposive approach 49, 51, 53, 63–4

quashing order 106
Queen: Orders in Council 41
Queen's Bench 88
Queen's Bench Divisional Court
	(QBD) 106, 131
Queen's Council (QC) 148
Queen's Speech 37

ratio decidendi 9, 16, 17
recorders 156, 157
rehabilitation 139
Renton Committee 38
reparation orders 139–40
reparation/restitution, sentencing as
	139–40

repeal of Acts of Parliament 44
reprimand/warning 143
restriction orders 143
retribution *see* punishment
Royal Assent (of Bill) 39
Royal Commissions 86

Salmond, J. 1
samples 117–18, 119, 124
    indefinite retention of 118
searches
    of premises 111–12, 119, 121–2
    samples and fingerprinting
        117–18
    stop and search 110, 119,
        120–1
    warrants 111, 130
secrecy of jury room 174–5, 183,
        187–9
sentencing 136
    aims of 137
    denunciation 140
    deterrence 138
    factors surrounding offence
        143–4
    Magistrates' Court 134
    mentally ill offenders 143
    offender's background 144
    other powers of court 142
    protection of society 138–9
    rehabilitation 139
    reparation or restitution 139–40
    types of 140–2
    see also punishment; young
        offenders
Sentencing Council guidelines 144
separation of powers doctrine 158
silence, right to 116
Simonds, Lord 54
small claims track 88, 90
    appeals 91–2
'soft law' 76
solicitors 146–7

advocacy rights 147
    duty of care 151–2
    duty solicitor scheme 193
    Law Society 146, 149, 150
    private funding in civil cases 192
    public funding in civil cases
        190–2
    Queen's Council (QC) 148
    role 146–7
    suing (negligent advocacy) 150,
        152–3
    training 146
sources of law
    classification by 3–4
    European Union law 73–4, 78,
        79–82
stare decisis 8
statutory instruments 41, 42–3
statutory interpretation 48
    approaches to 49–50
    European approach 49, 53
    extrinsic aids 51–2, 56, 65–8
    and Human Rights Act 1998 54
    intrinsic aids 51
    judicial role in 54–5
    need for 49
    presumptions 53
    purposive approach 49, 51, 53,
        63–4
    rules
        Golden Rule 50, 52, 58–60
        of language 52, 56, 68–70
        Literal Rule 50, 52, 56–8
        Mischief Rule 50, 52, 60–2
statutory law 3
stop and search powers 110, 119,
        120–1
strip search 117
'success fee' 192
suing
    judicial immunity 159
    lawyers 150, 151, 152–3
summary offences 129

superior judges 156, 157, 159
Supreme Court 10, 11, 13, 158
    appeals from Crown Court 132
    appeals from Magistrates' Court
        131
    and Court of Appeal 14–15, 18,
        133–4
    Justices 156
    multi-track civil appeals 92
    Practice Rules 10, 13
    tribunals 104

tape-recorded interviews 116
temporary commissions/committees
    86
time limits
    civil cases 96, 98
    detention at police station 115
training
    barristers 147–8
    judiciary 157
    lay magistrates 165
    solicitors 146
Treaties (EU) 75
Treaty of Rome 54, 72
triable either way offences 129, 130

tribunals 103
    administrative 103
    advantages and disadvantages
        105
    composition and procedure
        104–5
    control of 105–6
    domestic 106–7
    First Tier 104
    history of 104
    unified system 104
    Upper 104

ultra vires doctrine 42, 43

Watch Committee 108
White Papers 37
Woolf, Lord/Woolf Review 86, 90

young offenders
    custodial sentences 141
    fines 142
    other powers of courts 142–3
Youth Court 130
youth offender team, referral to 143
youth rehabilitation orders 142–3